Worldy Amusements

Restoring the Lordship of Christ to Our Entertainment Choices

Wayne A. Wilson

WINEPRESS WP PUBLISHING

ISBN 1-57921-213-1
Library of Congress Catalog Card Number: 99-60171

For Laura,
my excellent wife,
passionate partner in marriage,
model of modesty in the world,
and a true disciple
of the Lord Jesus Christ

Acknowledgments

I owe a tremendous thanks to many brothers and sisters in Christ, who not only encouraged the writing of this book, but helped shape it through long discussion, criticism, and suggestions.

Faithful friends prayed this book to completion. My love and respect for these people knows no bounds. A few, most directly involved in the process, deserve special mention.

- Sue Cull, who brought order out of syntactical chaos. She not only brought coherence to my sentences, laboring many hours with the early manuscript, she added ideas I had not considered, but welcomed gladly.
- Paul Swift, a local artist, who believed enough in the message of the book to donate his talents in creating and designing the engaging cover art.

- Sol Brodsky, steadfast friend and kindred spirit, who cares deeply about this issue. Involved in many ways at every stage, Sol affirmed my belief that the church needs these ideas. His ability to ask hard questions made me defend every point, scripturally and logically.
- Dr. John MacArthur, who gave early encouragement with the project, and taught me, from the time I began my walk with Christ, to let Scripture be my guide always.
- Jim Bray, from Westside Bible Church, who read the early draft "hot off the printer," made helpful suggestions, and encouraged the effort.
- Art and Randee Trouville, dear friends, whose prayers sustain many worthwhile things, including anything worthy in this book.
- My brother elders at Acton Faith Bible Church, Mel Abel and Shawn Caldwell, who let me give many hours to the project and helped fill the gap.
- My parents, who always encouraged me to follow my dreams, even when it meant turning the house into a movie studio!
- Most of all, my wife Laura and my children, who had to put up with many hours of Dad laboring over the book, but never complained.

Contents

Quislings in the Church

This is one book that never should have been written. It should not have been written because it should not have been necessary. It is necessary. My subject is the Christian and entertainment. My contention is that we have grown too close to the world. Every Christian seems to agree that we live in a time of cultural decline. Obscenity, vulgarity, and perversion are the norms. Decency, honor, and purity are the exceptions.

Christians talk about "culture war" as though it were an Us-versus-Them contest. I will argue that we are the enemy—that it is Us versus Us. The decadence prevails because it is largely funded by Christian dollars, viewed in Christian homes, and welcomed by Christian hearts. Somehow we have grown fond of the world. Christians have always been tempted by the world, but this is, I believe, the first generation of Bible-believing Christians ever to have embraced evil amusements so completely. We delight in that which is an offense to our God. Because we love what the world loves, the world is tearing us down.

A few examples:

- A noted evangelical congressman is concerned about his colleagues sexual temptations, which seem to come with the pressures of living in Washington. "All the sexual stuff is hitting all my friends who are between 40 and 45," he says. "It seems like they're all losing their minds over it, and I think I'm susceptible to that too." To help them, he forms a prayer group and they often socialize, going to ball games and a weekly movie. One film they've seen is *The Devil's Advocate*, a hard R-rated film containing abundant nudity and explicit sexual scenes. This is to help promote fidelity.

- The most well-known Christian singer in America lends her singing talents to the very R-rated movie *The Postman*, featuring nudity and sexual activity as entertainment.

- Last year church leaders across the land encouraged their flocks and youth groups to see *Titanic*, a film that glorified teenage sexual immorality, simply because the film (unfairly) condemned the rich.

- A church in southern California uses video clips from current Hollywood movies as sermon illustrations, including crude and tasteless Jim Carrey movies. This technique, while creative, puts the stamp of approval on Hollywood right in the sanctuary.

- An evangelical seminary sponsored a film festival in 1994 and used, as a means "to stimulate and challenge our individual praying, thinking, feeling, and doing," the showing of numerous hard R-rated films, such as *Blade Runner*, *American Gigolo*, and *Boyz in the Hood*, among others.

- A writing workshop was conducted in southern California for Christians. Christian radio advertised as its special, featured speakers a married couple responsible for the morally sleazy *Batman Forever*. Celebrity status alone put forth these professed Christians as models of success to be emulated by Christians entering the entertainment profession.

What is going on here? Can anything be stranger than all of this? Can anyone even imagine anything like these things occurring among Christian leaders in any previous age? Not very long ago any one of these items would have been a cause for scandal in any Christian denomination or local body of believers.

Forgetting Whose Side We're On

During the Second World War, the Germans sought to use people in occupied lands as agents of their tyranny. In Norway, such collaborators were called "quislings"—named after the traitorous Norwegian who helped Hitler conquer his country. A quisling, naturally, was about as low as a person could sink in the eyes of his countrymen. By analogy, I am addressing the church on the subject of collaboration with the enemy. The enemy, in this case, is the ministry of propaganda for the worst tyrant known to man, the one C. S. Lewis's fictional demon Screwtape (in *The Screwtape Letters*) called "Our Father Below." If Satan loves impurity, indecency, and shamelessness, then surely modern Hollywood is one of his true allies.

Our enemy has created a glamorous, global, ubiquitous force for the corruption of souls. The whole world listens as it speaks, sending in dollars by the billions to sustain it, and receiving benefits from it that do not last, but that leave one hungry for more. In response, the church has fallen remarkably silent about this propaganda machine. When it does speak, the church whines about the enemy, yet remains fearful to challenge its own members for supporting it. Or in true quisling fashion, many in the church look for the positive in the face of this tyranny. *Yes*, the quisling thinks, *it twists us and our children, but what can one do? It is not so unpleasant if one learns to appreciate its finer points. We must learn to live with it.* In short, we compromise.

It is a difficult thing to live in enemy-occupied territory. It is hard to see the signs of tyranny surrounding us. The little space left free from the tyrant gets smaller and smaller, as his power—called sin—presses in upon us. Far more painful than the presence of our enemy is the support and comfort given to him by our own. If it is the church that gives legitimacy to wickedness through sustained patronage, and if indeed, hell is supported on the shoulders of God's people, somebody must sound the alarm.

Are Christians guilty of collaboration? My analogy of living in enemy-occupied territory is valid only if Hollywood's product is substantially evil. My use of the idea of collaboration is valid only if Christians do, in fact, support the evil products Hollywood generates. I will accept the burden in this book to explain why Christians should regard the vast majority of Hollywood's product as morally evil. I will do this by setting forth the biblical standard. If the church accepts that standard, Hollywood will become something to be shunned by Christians as detestable, rather than embraced for its allure.

As for evidence of collaboration, I would ask the reader to examine his own viewing habits, as well as those of Christian acquaintances. Beyond this, I will try to point out how much collaboration exists at the leadership levels of evangelicalism. My purpose is not to attack anyone but to spark earnest discussion among Christians and perhaps others sympathetic to a biblical morality.

Taking Aim

I am writing to the church, particularly my fellow evangelicals, who already know that we are not to be conformed to this world. I write to those who desire to live the Beatitudes of Jesus: those who have poverty of spirit; who grieve over sin in themselves and in the world around them; who are tamed into gentleness by God's grace; who feel the pangs of hunger as they seek righteousness above all else; who show mercy; and who seek purity of heart, unstained by the ways of the world. I am writing out of love and a burden of sadness. I seek to reprove, not condemn. My hope is that all who will read these pages will heed the wisdom of Solomon:

> Give instruction to a wise man, and he will be still wiser.
> Teach a righteous man, and he will increase his learning.
> (Prov. 9:9)

My goal is to shed biblical light on an area of Christian practice that has brought great harm to the cause of Christ.

I do mention in these pages a number of prominent Christians, because I believe leadership has played a decisive role in the compromise of the last twenty years. I will challenge the views and practices of brothers and sisters who have publicly taken a position on behalf of what I believe is severe moral compromise. I'm sure they do not believe it is compromise; that is the reason for this book. I would hope to persuade them, and you, to look at these issues once more. As I address the failures of leadership, I do so with love; if I wound anyone, I do so as a friend and a brother. By leadership, I mean popular Christian teachers and publications; outspoken Hollywood professionals; and Christian celebrities, who by virtue of their fame have a voice of authority even in the church.

It is important to note that the concept of celebrity is largely a phenomenon of modern times—a fascinating, if disturbing, part of the world in which we find ourselves. The pervasive influence of celebrity on the church needs the attention of a thoughtful writer somewhere. I became aware of this some twenty years ago as I sat around a table in the library of the film school I attended, sharing Christ with some fellow students. A Christian girl happened by and joined in immediately. Certain that I had missed the most persuasive point in favor of accepting the gospel, she said, "Lots of famous people are Christians," and she delineated a list of low-level Hollywood celebrities. After all, how could one hope to persuade someone else of truth without its endorsement by the beautiful people?

The Spirit of the Age

The church of Jesus Christ has challenges in every age. Some of the challenges are constant and unchanging: fulfilling the Great Commission, bringing biblical order to chaotic, immoral cultures, healing the broken, fighting heresy, and enduring the wrath of the ungodly. Each era faces many of the same challenges because people do not change. Humanity operates out of idolatry, lust, greed, and cruelty. These principles repeat themselves from generation to generation.

And yet there are different challenges from age to age, century to century. The German word *Zeitgeist* refers to the "the spirit of the time" and helps label the unique features of a given era. The church's success can be measured, not only by how well it contends with the unchanging challenges of human nature, but also by how well it addresses the spirit of the age.

Historical epochs differ. In the early church, the challenge was paganism. The church won that battle, though it may have assimilated too much from the opposition along the way. In the Middle Ages, the challenge was barbarism. Although there were minor successes in limiting human cruelty, the church largely adopted the spirit of the age, encouraging a violent, crusading zeal completely opposed to New Testament doctrine and morality. The Reformation successfully challenged the layers of tradition obscuring the gospel. But the church struggled in efforts to respond to the Enlightenment, a time when human reason was exalted over revelation. The last century produced the triple threat of Darwin, Marx, and Freud, all of whom are currently up against the ropes as history and science move beyond them.

And so we come to the end of the twentieth century and the beginning of the third millennium. Our time has been called, sadly but I think truly, the "Age of Show Business." While young hearts used to thrill to the experiences of great explorers, scientists, missionaries, government leaders, and soldiers, today the loyalty of all ages seems directed to music groups and movie stars. This is a global phenomenon. Show people—once a suspect class of people kept on society's margins—now reign supreme as idols, stars, and royalty. Their advice is sought on every conceivable subject. They testify before congress on issues they know about only because they were in a movie. Unfortunately, celebrity worship knows no national boundaries. A young Iraqi friend once told me how deeply loved Elvis Presley was in his country. All I could think of to ask was, "Why?"

"He is beautiful," the young man explained. "He is like angel . . . like a god!" It is moments like these that make life a parody of itself.

What does a Christian do in the Age of Show Business? Are there any moral imperatives?

What do we do with the scriptural admonition "Do not love the world, nor the things in the world" (1 John 2:15a)?

How do we apply this when the world crowds in on us with images and language wholly devoted to "the lust of the flesh, the lust of the eyes, and the boastful pride of life" (v. 16b)? I hope to suggest some answers to these questions. With the words of Martin Luther, let me encourage you to keep reading:

> If I profess with the loudest voice and with the clearest exposition every portion of the truth of God except that little point which the world and the devil are at that moment attacking, I am not professing Christ, however boldly I proclaim I am professing Christ. Where the battle rages, there the loyalty of the soldier is proved. No matter how steady on all fronts beside, it is mere flight and disgrace if he flinches at that vital point.[1]

In the Age of Show Business, one vital point is how we choose to amuse ourselves. Our enemy advances through Hollywood. Where are you? In the fight, on the sidelines, or openly collaborating? Read on with an open heart and mind. Our Prince calls us to the battle.

Before proceeding, I must warn you. This book focuses a lot on sex and related topics. Worldliness certainly includes many attitudes and practices that don't involve sex, but the purity issue is by far the most pressing when it comes to Hollywood. I could have written about Hollywood's Christian-bashing, but Michael Medved has addressed that topic better than I ever could. K. L. Billingsley handles the subject of politics well in his book *The Seductive Image*. I could have written about the attitudes of children in movies, the false idols of beauty and celebrity, or the false religious hopes of science fiction. (I once preached a sermon on science-fiction saviors after Jodie Foster's movie-version of *Contact* came out.) These concepts are easily discussed and even may be doors for evangelism. I frequently use *Star Wars* to help explain the difference between eastern religion and Christianity. Discernment and instruction can be employed against error.

While false ideas can be fought with true ideas, impurity fights in a different arena, for purity is about more than ideas. Immoral images and words cannot be explained away. They are presented directly to the soul, working damage that rational and moral explanations cannot alter. For this reason I will focus on impurity, because that is Hollywood's most devastating curse on the land.

I have found it an unpleasant experience to write so extensively on this subject. Thinking about immorality on this scale leaves one feeling beat up, yet all the more aware of how the soul cannot help but be affected by the content of so many movies. Yet, if Christians and their leaders begin to examine entertainment issues seriously from a biblical perspective, it will have been worth much worse than what I have put myself through.

I have a final request of you, the reader. This book was written with much prayer. I would ask the reader to reflect upon it prayerfully as well.

Chapter Two

What Are Worldly Amusements?

Worldly amusements are just what the name suggests. They are amusements, or entertainment, that do at least one (or both) of the following:

1. They promote an *evil message*. In this case the entertainment presents evil as a good. This can be done by celebrating sins, such as lying, stealing, fornication, adultery, or even, in the case of *Silence of the Lambs*, murder and cannibalism. Sin is presented in an attractive way.

2. They use *evil methods*. Regardless of the point of the story, the performers are made to behave in ways that are shameless and immoral. A story may lead to the conclusion that adultery is bad, but if we must wal-

low through a sea of flesh to reach this conclusion, the work certainly qualifies as worldly.

Evil message. Evil method. Defining worldly amusements this way simply follows the Bible's definition given in 1 John 2:16. They appeal to the lust of the flesh, the lust of the eyes, and the boastful pride of life. Worldly amusements are an illicit means of recreation. They give pleasure but violate Christian moral teaching to do so.

In preparing this book, I sought to use a different term than *worldly amusements*. The term is associated in my mind with a legalistic approach to Christian recreation, which seems overly harsh and narrow. But in the end, I found the term to be a good one. It describes well what I am talking about and what I hope the church will begin to talk about once again.

Worldly amusements traditionally have included things such as playing cards, gambling, going to the theater, dancing, and the like. They were things that the church looked upon as promoting sin. Modern Christians look back and laugh. We are so proud of having broken away from those restrictions of the past. But what are we laughing at? Are we laughing from a position of greater sophistication? Does the average Christian know the Bible better than those earlier generations? Would our spiritual life be characterized as more mature? Are we more pure? More godly? More devoted to prayer? More willing to sacrifice for the kingdom? I think not. Our laughter really seems to come from a heart that wants to maximize personal liberty. We want to be very close to the world—indistinguishable from it. We want to enjoy nearly everything the world enjoys but with Jesus added on as Savior.

The Shifting Standard

Part of the problem is that the world has taken such a drastic cultural downturn. Things that once were condemned seem relatively minor now. For the modern Christian, taking illegal drugs is worldliness. Such things as promiscuous sexual practices, strip clubs, and hard-core pornography are defined as worldly because now they are open dangers, whereas in generations past, these were relatively unknown or hidden evils. Compared to all of this, network television and PG-13 movies seem rather mild. But they are not.

It is a mistake to define "mild" evils by comparison with our culture's greatest deficiencies. When the church does that, Christian standards also decline. We live to a lower standard than previous generations because we measure ourselves by the bottom, and the bottom keeps sinking lower. As long as we are above the most degenerate evils, we feel holy. But if we could look back, we would see that we have fallen, in our moral lives, below the level of many unbelievers when the common culture was governed by a Christian ethic. This is wrong. We need to look up.

Our standard should be the Bible's standard. It should be a consistent standard across the ages. I am not speaking of culturally variant issues. I am talking about universal standards of decency regarding modesty, speech, and thought life. These are biblical principles that believers from every culture must embrace. Modesty is a universal principle for believers. Lust is an evil across cultures. Respecting women as sisters is a Christian command, not a colloquial practice of 1950s America. If it means anything to be a Christian, it should mean desiring to live as Jesus did. It is His perspective we should have; His approval we should seek.

There are, according to Jesus, two paths to walk. One is wide, and it leads to destruction. The other, which leads to life, is narrow. The righteous are supposed to walk the narrow path. Unfortunately, many Christians have embarked on a road-improvement program. Trees are being felled, hillsides blasted, the shoulder paved. We labor hard to widen the road, when all we're supposed to do is walk it. The casual acceptance of immoral entertainment is one way we try to widen God's narrow way.

The Scope of This Work

The worldly amusements under consideration in this book are almost exclusively products of Hollywood. The simple reason for this is that I know this area. Popular music has held no attraction for me since I was a child, and I don't know anything about it. The movies I know. I know their power. And I believe that our entertainment choices are among the greatest contributors to moral compromise in modern times. We *are* being harmed by this compromise in a thousand ways.

As a pastor, I am tired of learning which of our teens has lost his or her virginity this week. I have grown weary of hearing a teen tell me about the "tasteful" nudity in a film, such as *Schindler's List*, and a few months later turn up pregnant. Physical purity for the modern young person is not easily maintained. It is the exception, not the rule. Biblical standards would not be satisfied with mere physical purity if we could achieve it. Christians, young and old, are to labor for pure hearts and pure minds! Pastors everywhere should say to impure entertainment, "Enough is enough!" We should reclaim the desire of the apostle who wrote, "I want you to be wise in what is good, and innocent in what is evil" (Rom. 16:19).

If we picture moral innocence as a finely woven fabric, then we should understand that every naughty joke in a movie is a snag in that material. Every nude scene is a pulled thread; every fornicating couple, a tear; and every sexual act witnessed, a slash. Soon, and it doesn't take long, that fine material is as shredded as a battle flag carried through Pickett's Charge. Moral innocence is in shambles. We should not be surprised that it is not successfully maintained. Our amusements have taught us not to regard moral innocence as precious.

The church has always seen worldly amusements as a threat to the soul. It is our arrogance that dismisses the wisdom of the ages. I sit on a committee in our fellowship that examines young men who desire to go into the ministry. I have noticed that many young pastors have little regard for history. They are not familiar with the counsel of Christ's ministers of the past. They are disturbingly ignorant of lessons learned long ago that have been affirmed time after time. The church of the third millennium will be impoverished by this ignorance. I challenge you not to skip over the next chapter. It is long, and the language is difficult, but it is the wisdom of men who were given by Christ to lead His church.

Chapter Three

What Does the Church Say?

Church history is a subject near to my heart. Most of the problems and heresies the church faces today have been around before. How the church handled issues in the past, though not binding, is always instructive. The New Testament speaks of church leaders as Christ's gifts to the church (see Eph. 4:11–13) Because we have centuries of wisdom and experience behind us, we are fools to ignore those voices which, though now gone, are not silent. The past reveals our present condition. If we are out of sync with every previous generation, we should at least ask ourselves why. Only arrogance ignores the past.

The movie business has been around for only a century, but any examination of the church's relationship with Hollywood must reach back before Edison's camera, to include a look at the art form that is most like film: the theater.

The Early Church

Christianity was born into the Roman world, an environment in which the theater arts were widely practiced and enjoyed. Roman-style theaters were built even in Palestine during the first century. By the time Christians wrote concerning the theater, Roman plays had degenerated into low comedies, vulgar miming, and sensual displays of women. The moral tone was very much like that of network television in our day. Historian Philip Schaff says the theater was once a school of public morals in Greece, but the moralistic plays grew tiresome for the Romans, whose tastes had been brought to the most base level by the bloody thrills of the arena and the circus.[1]

The stage prospered, but the quality declined. Stars of the stage were extremely well paid and the center of attention at social affairs. Women threw themselves at noted actors, and female performers were often taunted into sensual behavior by the audiences.[2] It should come as no surprise that the early church restricted the theaters, along with the games, on pain of excommunication. Baptism was denied to regular theater goers.

The reason for the hard stand is explained by the second-century theologian Tertullian:

> But if we ought to abominate all that is immodest, on what ground is it right to hear what we must not speak? For all licentiousness of speech, nay, every idle word, is

condemned by God. Why, in the same way, is it right to look on what it is disgraceful to do? How is it that the things which defile a man going out of his mouth, are not regarded as doing so when they go in at his eyes and ears— when eyes and ears are the immediate attendants on the spirit—and that can never be pure whose servants-in-waiting are impure? You have the theater forbidden, then, in the forbidding of immodesty.[3]

His argument is essentially that of the church in all ages until our own. Corrupt speech and immodest performances do harm to the spirit and defile the purity of the Christian. It is true that Tertullian disapproved of much, and there are those who point to his excesses as reason to ignore him, but his arguments against the theater have near-unanimous support through all the ages of church history.

Menucius Felix, a third-century father, connected the gladiatorial violence with the immodest theater, labeling both as evil pleasures:

We therefore, who are estimated by our character and our modesty, reasonably abstain from evil pleasures, and from your pomps and exhibitions, the origin of which in connection with sacred things we know, and condemn their mischievous enticements. For in the chariot games who does not shudder at the madness of the people brawling among themselves? Or at the teaching of murder in the gladiatorial games? In the scenic games also [theater] the madness is not less, but the debauchery is more prolonged: for now a mimic either expounds or shows forth adulteries; now a nervous player, while he feigns lust, suggests it;

the same actor disgraces your gods by attributing to them adulteries, sighs, hatreds; the same provokes your tears with pretended sufferings, with vain gestures and expressions. Thus you demand murder, in fact, while you weep at it in fiction.[4]

The actor, he points out, "while he feigns lust, suggests it." This comment could certainly be made of the majority of Hollywood's product, from PG films right on up.

Cyprian, the bishop of Carthage and a martyr, wrote at length on this subject. His words on the popular Roman mimes deserve careful consideration:

> But now to pass from this to the shameless corruption of the stage. I am ashamed to tell what things are said; I am even ashamed to denounce the things that are done— the tricks of arguments, the cheatings of adulterers, the immodesties of women, the scurrile jokes, the sordid parasites, even the toga'd fathers of families themselves, sometimes stupid, sometimes obscene, but in all cases dull, in all cases immodest. And though no individual, or family, or profession, is spared by the discourse of these reprobates, yet everyone flocks to the play. The general infamy is delightful to see or to recognize; it is a pleasure, nay, even to learn it. People flock thither to the public disgrace of the brothel for the teaching of obscenity, that nothing less may be done in secret than what is learnt in public; and in the midst of the laws themselves is taught everything that the laws forbid.
>
> What does a faithful Christian do among these things, since he may not even think upon wickedness? Why does

he find pleasure in the representations of lust, so as among them to lay aside his modesty and become more daring in crimes? He is learning to do, while he is becoming accustomed to see. Nevertheless, those women whom their misfortune has introduced and degraded to this slavery, conceal their public wantonness, and find consolation for their disgrace in their concealment. Even they who have sold their modesty blush to appear to have done so. But that public prodigy is transacted in the sight of all, and the obscenity of prostitutes is surpassed. A method is sought to commit adultery with the eyes.

To this infamy an infamy fully worthy of it is superadded: a human being broken down in every limb, a man melted to something beneath the effeminacy of a woman, has found the art to supply language with his hands; and on behalf of one—I know not what, but neither man nor woman—the whole city is in a state of commotion, that the fabulous debaucheries of antiquity may be presented in the ballet. Whatever is not lawful is so beloved, that what had even been lost sight of by the lapse of time is brought back again into the recollection of the eyes.[5]

Cyprian engages the reader with powerful observations. Several themes emerge: the theater's tendency to destroy shame and modesty in the patrons; the instruction in immorality by its representation—"He is learning to do, while being accustomed to see"; and the degraded condition of the performers. All of these issues cast before the Christian this question: "What does the faithful Christian do among these things, since he may not even think upon wickedness?" This question must be asked today and it deserves a serious answer.

Can you handle a few more church fathers? Don't give up yet! You need to understand how universal was this opinion of the theater's dangers. Let's go on. Lactantius, tutor to Constantine's son Crispus, demonstrates that in the fourth century, the concerns expressed two hundred years previous were no less real.

> What of the stage? Is it more holy,—on which comedy converses on the subject of debaucheries and amours, tragedy of incest and parricide? The immodest gestures also of the players, with which they imitate disreputable women, teach the lusts, which they express by dancing. For the pantomime is a school of corruption, in which things which are shameful are acted by a figurative representation, that the things which are true may be done without shame. These spectacles are viewed by youths, whose dangerous age, which ought to be curbed and governed, is trained by these representations to vices and sins.
>
> The circus, in truth, is considered more innocent, but there is greater madness in this, since the minds of the spectators are transported with such great madness, that they not only break out into revilings, but often rise to strifes, and battles, and contentions. Therefore all shows are to be avoided, that we may be able to maintain a tranquil state of mind. We must renounce hurtful pleasures, lest, charmed by pestilential sweetness, we fall into the snares of death.[6]

By this time, the violent sports of the circus are considered "more innocent" than the theater, but it is still an assault on the tranquility of the Christian spirit. Notice, too, that each of the fathers recognizes the pleasurable aspects of these worldly amusements. They are fun. They offer a kind of "sweetness," but they lead to moral disaster.

You may have noticed that each of these men mentions the virtue of modesty in condemning these amusements. There is a tendency in our time to dismiss the early fathers moral instruction because they were "obsessive" about pagan religion. Everything was forbidden because it was somehow connected to the gods. While that is a concern in their writings, it is not the main concern in this issue or in many others. The fathers were not single-minded against paganism; they were single-minded for Christ. That means they challenged and exposed evil in its varied forms. Idolatry was one concern. An angry, violent spirit was another; the devaluation of life in the arena, another; immodest theater, still another.

The fourth-century powerhouse, John Chrysostom, was bishop of Constantinople. A zealous reformer of abuses in the church, he earned the name Golden Mouth because of his great preaching. In an extended discussion of the need for self-control among the young, he proclaimed:

"Follow after peace . . . and the sanctification, without which no man shall see the Lord" (Heb. 12:4). Is not this threat sufficient to terrify you? Do you see others continuing altogether in chastity, and in gravity passing their lives; and cannot you command yourself even so long as the period of youth? Do you see others ten thousand times overcoming pleasure, and cannot you once refrain? With your leave I will tell you the cause,—for youth is not the cause, since then all men would be dissolute. But we thrust ourselves into the fire. For when you go up to the theater, and sit feasting your eyes with the naked limbs of women, for the time indeed you are delighted, but afterwards, you have nourished there a mighty fever. When you see women exhibited as it were in the form of their bodies, and spectacles and songs containing nothing else but irregular loves . . . tell me, how will you be able to continue chaste afterwards, these narratives, these spectacles, these songs occupying your soul, and dreams of this sort henceforth succeeding.[7]

These are the words of frontline Christianity in the age of emperors. These are the men who met paganism and worldliness head on, as a persecuted minority, and triumphed. These are men of the church who understood what was going on in the world. And to the immodest theatrics of the ancient world—certainly less explicit in some ways than modern entertainment—they said no.

The Middle Ages

The ancient theater eventually declined under the rise of Christian civilization. It took a long time to come back. But in the high Middle Ages, the church increasingly employed pageantry and a kind of liturgical drama to communicate Christian truth to an illiterate populace. Eventually, these dramas developed into the mystery plays and morality plays, which sought to communicate divine truth and

Christian morals through a rough-and-tumble, often comedic style. The drama became too wild for the church and moved, by stages, into the street, where it blended with the simple theatrics of minstrel shows and mime groups. After a time, as the Renaissance came on and a love of all things classical was renewed, the secular theater made a comeback in the sixteenth century.

The Reformers were quite used to the presence of theater in their world. Where Reformation principles were in the ascendancy, mystery plays were repressed for theological reasons, as expressions of Catholicism, not as drama, per se. In England, under Henry VIII, Protestant plays were put on to discourage faith in the old church. In Germany, Luther was asked about religious plays and answered that they should be allowed, since plays of that kind were "harmless customs" and "inoffensive." Theodore Beza, John Calvin's close friend and successor, was a poet before his conversion, and afterward he put his creative gifts into God's service. His play *Abraham Sacrifant* was performed in Geneva, went through many French editions, and was widely translated.[8]

Morally speaking, early secular theater—Shakespeare included—could be verbally suggestive and rough. Though nothing close to a typical, comedy-club routine or R-rated movie of today, it was vulgar at times. Since secular theater had a profit motive, an appeal to all tastes and classes was attempted. Thus, lofty themes and thoughtful characterizations were mixed with low humor to amuse the masses. But in terms of action, the theater had to be essentially modest. Women's parts were played by men in the early years, and male and female characters never so much as embraced. (It is an achievement of modern cinema to force sex scenes into Shakespeare!)

Biblical Protestantism did not appreciate the classical revival of worldly amusements. In England, the Puritans vigorously opposed the theater for numerous reasons, many of which were delineated by William Prynne in his *Histriomastix* in 1633. This work so provoked King Charles I that he had Prynne's ears chopped off!

Prynne listed many legitimate means of recreation for the Christian and included in that list the reading and writing of plays. However, staging a play, for Prynne and other Puritans, was an entirely different matter. One of the main concerns was the moral lives of the performers. In Prynne's day, men played the female roles generally, which violated the Bible's law on cross-dressing and promoted homosexuality. At the same time, Prynne reasoned, if women were put in female roles, the performers would likely be tempted into fornication and adultery. Bruce Daniels points out:

> To some extent reality justified these criticisms. Sexual themes coursed through many plays and an easy sexuality, homosexual as well as heterosexual, often characterized the lives of actors and abounded in theater districts.[9]

The issue of sexual temptations brought to the performers through their participation in worldly productions is a forgotten issue in the modern church, but it too needs to be revisited in a serious way.

Prynne thought the theater waged war on Christian modesty for performers and audience alike. Christian purity was scandalized by "wanton gestures, amorous kisses, lascivious whorish actions, the beautiful faces . . . the witty obsceni-ties." Of course, theater in Prynne's day was much more mild than modern Hollywood, but the danger was clear. How could such antics on stage be viewed as acceptable in the light of the Bible's teaching on the mind's proper dwelling place, the pure heart, and edifying speech?

Puritan Richard Baxter asked:

Hath God given you such a world of lawful pleasures, and will none of them, nor all of them, serve your turns, with-out unlawful ones, or at least unfit ones (which therefore are unlawful): all these are undoubtedly lawful; but cards, and dice, and stage-plays are, at best, very questionable: among wise and learned men, and good men, and no small number of these, they are condemned as unlawful. And should one that feareth God and loveth his salvation, choose so doubtful a sport, before such an abundance of undoubtedly lawful ones?

Responding to the man who asks, "Why should I leave my sport for another man's conceits or judgments?" Baxter says,

I will tell thee that which will shame thy reply, and thee, if thou canst blush. It is not some humorous, odd fanatic that I allege against thee, nor a singular divine; but it is the judgment of the ancient church itself. The fathers and councils condemn Christians and ministers especially, that use *spectacula*, spectacles, or behold stage-plays or dicing.[10]

So strong was the Puritan feeling against the theater, that the first plays staged in America did not come about until the mid-eighteenth century! Every English colony, including many non-Puritan settlements, disallowed the theater for all of the seventeenth century and most of the eighteenth.

The Modern Eras

During the Enlightenment, the theater took a definite turn toward the bawdy and the lewd, as can be evidenced by Voltaire's witty but impure themes. The French scientist and thinker Blaise Pascal, a strong Christian, spoke pointedly about the theater and its dangers in his *Pensees*. To Pascal, the theater was a formidable obstacle to the Christian life.

All great amusements are dangerous to the Christian life, but among all those the world has invented, there is none more to be feared than the theater. It is a representation of the passions so natural and so delicate, that it excites them and gives birth to them in our hearts—and above all, to that of love, principally when it is represented as very chaste and virtuous. For the more innocent it appears to innocent souls, the more they are likely to be touched by it. Its violence pleases our self-love, which immediately forms a desire to produce the same effects that we see being so well represented. At the same time, we make ourselves a conscience founded on the propriety of the feelings we see there, by which the fear of pure souls is removed, since they imagine that it cannot hurt their purity to love with a love that seems to them so reasonable.

So we depart from the theater, with our heart so filled with all the beauty and tenderness of love, the soul and the mind so persuaded of its innocence, that we are quite ready to receive its first impressions or, rather, seek an opportunity of awakening them in the heart of another, that we may receive the same pleasures and the same sacrifices we have seen so well represented in the theater.[11]

Pascal's Jansenist pietism and attentive mind was very sensitive to the idea of manipulation by the theater. What we see in the theater changes us. It prioritizes emotions. It puts in us ideas and, most of all, feelings that would not have been there otherwise. It shapes our view of life. Pascal does not settle for blasting the lascivious. Even innocent love in the play creates in us the subtle desire to have what we have seen, even if that means using or manipulating someone else to get it for ourselves or, possibly, submitting ourselves to an unhealthy situation in order to have it. His concern certainly deserves consideration in any discussion of the cinema, a more powerful art form than the stage.

In England, the great preachers and Christian activists—people who fought epic battles on issues of major importance, did not neglect to comment on the theater. William Wilberforce, the dedicated opponent of the slave trade, wrote in his very popular book:

The Stage.—I am well aware, that I am now about to tread on very tender ground; but it would be an improper deference to the opinions and manners of the age, altogether to avoid it. There has been much argument concerning the lawfulness of theatrical amusements. Let it be sufficient to remark, that the controversy would be short indeed, if the question were to be tried by this criterion of love to the Supreme Being. If there were anything of that sensibility for the honor of God, and of that zeal in His service, which we show in behalf of our earthly friends, or of our political connections, should we seek our pleasure in that place which the debauchee, inflamed with wine, or bent on the gratification of other licentious appetites, finds most congenial to his state and temper of mind? In that place, from the neighborhood of which, (how justly termed 'a school of morals' might hence alone be inferred,) decorum, and modesty, and regularity retire, while riot and lewdness are invited to the spot, and invariably select it for their chosen residence! Where the sacred name of God is often profaned! Where sentiments are often heard with delight, and motions and gestures often applauded, which would not be tolerated in private company, but which may far exceed the utmost license allowed in the social circle, without at all transgressing the large bounds of theatrical decorum! Where, when moral principles are inculcated, they are not such as a Christian ought to cherish in his bosom, but such as it must be his daily endeavor to extirpate; not those which Scripture warrants, but those which it condemns as false and spurious, being founded in pride and ambition, and the over-valuation of human favor! Where surely, if a Christian should trust himself at all, it would be requisite for him to prepare himself with a double portion of watchfulness and seriousness of mind, instead of selecting it as a place in which he may throw off his guard, and unbend without danger![12]

Mark well his concluding thought: An entertainment is where we relax, but a worldly entertainment is just the environment where we should be doubly on guard. If we must be so cautious in the midst of this evil, why are we there in the first place? Wilberforce was a man of the world before his conversion to Christ. He knew the world of which he wrote. To him, there were not great issues and small issues, but only issues of faith and morality. How does one's behavior fulfill the two great commandments as defined by Jesus: love God with all of your being, and your neighbor as yourself.

More cautious was Wilberforce's contemporary John Wesley, founder of the Methodist church. Trying to avoid making rules that were not firmly rooted in Scripture, Wesley withholds condemning the theater in broad terms, but does take a strong personal stand with regard to the English theater of the eighteenth century:

> We cannot be always intent upon business. Both our bodies and minds require some relaxation. We need intervals of diversion from business. It will be necessary to be very explicit upon this head, as it is a point which has been much misunderstood.
>
> Diversions are of various kinds. Some, which were formerly in great request, are now fallen into disrepute [such as hawking, broad-sword, quarterstaff, cudgeling, bear-baiting, bull-baiting]. It is not needful to say anything more of these foul remains of gothic barbarity, than that they are a reproach, not only to all religion, but even to human nature. One would not pass so severe a censure on the sports of the field. Let those who have nothing better to do, still run foxes and hares out of breath. Neither need

much be said about horse-races, til some man of sense
will undertake to defend them. It seems a great deal more
may be said in defense of seeing a serious tragedy. I could
not do it with a clear conscience; at least not in an English theater, the sink of all profaneness and debauchery;
but possibly others can. I cannot say quite so much for
balls and assemblies, which though more reputable than
masquerades, yet must be allowed by all impartial persons
to have exactly the same tendency. So undoubtedly have
all public dancings. Of playing at cards I say the same as
of seeing plays. I could not do it with a clear conscience.
But I am not obliged to pass any sentence on those that
are otherwise minded. I leave them to their own Master.
To Him let them stand or fall.[13]

Here we have a balanced, sound perspective from another
godly man. You can hear him laboring to be fair. He is careful to allow that theatrical works may not be evil, but those
of his time certainly were. It should be remembered that
actually openly performing sexual acts or displays of naked
bodies, as is common in entertainment attended by many
Christians in our day, was completely unthinkable. Wesley
is describing, at worst, teasing sexual themes, double
entendre, and the like—such as might appear in a typical
network television show, only less graphic. It is not difficult to imagine what Wesley would think about a James
Bond movie.

The Movies

The end of the nineteenth century saw the arrival of the
motion picture. Early films were trivial affairs, not drawing

much attention from clergy. One-minute films were run as oddities at sideshows or fairs. To keep up interest, subjects became more "sensational." One simply featured a couple discreetly kissing for one minute. Another featured a train rushing toward the camera, reportedly causing women to faint and others to flee the showroom in terror. Some innovators finally decided to do stories. The breakthrough film, which set cinema apart as its own art form, was *The Great Train Robbery* made in 1903.

Soon, ten-minute features (one reelers) were very popular. Film was rapidly becoming an art form to be reckoned with. *The Birth of a Nation*, made in 1915, was three hours long and had a full score played by a live orchestra. Woodrow Wilson said it "was like writing history in lightening." The film industry could not grow fast enough. The public started to identify with and idolize actors. Recognizing the power of promoting personalities, the studios forged the "star system" in the 1920s. Once it was realized that enormous amounts of money could be made with film, the introduction of "naughty" movies was close at hand. The titles gave away the themes of these films, among them *Beware, My Husband Comes*; *The Bigamist*; *Curse of True Love*; *College Boy's First Love*; and *Gaities of Divorce*.

Churches reacted strongly to these sleazy films, beginning a long-standing condemnation of the whole film industry, which lasted for many years. In 1920, a Christian lobbyist in Washington—a certain Dr. Craft—stated his goal to "rescue the motion pictures from the hands of the devil and 500 non-Christian Jews."[14] Despite Craft's anti-Semitic comment, Hollywood in the twenties really was "Sin City, USA."

Newspapers covered the lives of decadent movie stars, studio prostitution, and orgiastic parties. Arthur Knight explains how much the films themselves reflected this lifestyle:

> Hollywood in its films was reflecting the change in moral standards. Sophisticated sex had suddenly become big box-office, whether in comedies or played straight. Drinking scenes abounded in pictures, despite the recent adoption of Prohibition. Divorce, seduction, the use of drugs were presented in film after film as symbols of fashionable life. America was launched upon an era of high living, and Hollywood was pointing the way. But in towns and hamlets across the nation, the new morality had not taken hold. Many who went to the movies were genuinely shocked by what they saw there—and concluded that what they saw was representative of Hollywood alone.[15]

The introduction of sound at the end of the 1920s enhanced the movies, but themes continued in the same vein as before. Titles, such as *Virgin Paradise*, *Scrambled Wives*, and *Plaything of Broadway*, were typical. These movies were tame by today's standards, but they did reflect the free-and-easy sexual attitudes of the Roaring Twenties. A lot of skin was shown—mostly ladies in their underwear—and flashes of nudity were not uncommon. Early musicals found creative ways to titillate the audience with suggested nudity. Language remained suggestive rather than outright indecent. In those days everyone knew that there were words you didn't say in mixed company.

Hollywood drank deeply from the stream of deception and lies that has shaped twentieth-century sexuality. Freud, the prophet of psychoanalysis, taught that man's being was rooted in his sexuality. His ideas rapidly shaped (or perhaps simply justified) the rich, urban, secular culture which followed the Victorian era. Freud's ideas on sex dominated magazines, books, and theater in the second and third decades of this century. The freedom he championed received anthropological support from the young Margaret Mead, whose *Coming of Age in Somoa* (1928) became the justification for sexual freedom. In combination with women's rights, the closed automobile, and birth control, secular ideas on unrestrained sexuality pummeled the morals held to only a few years earlier. The movies were an instrument in that pummeling.

Sexual liberation, it turns out, was built on faulty data. Freud's theories are now discredited. Mead's work, used as anthropological gospel for decades, has been proven to be without scientific merit. These ideas were readily accepted, not because the work was so persuasive, but because humans are sinners. Many people found "scientific" support for the sexual freedom they craved, searing their own consciences.

Urban American culture was not as dominant then, and the church was still alive in both the cities and country. When the movies brought a godless and immoral culture into towns and communities that had been shaped by the Bible, Christians, along with many other decent people, fought hard for American civilization as they cherished it. Men of God preached a biblical standard and strongly discouraged movie attendance. With Congress under pressure to act, federal censorship looked like a very real possibility.

The Code

The movie industry panicked. In 1922, the MPPDA, an association of producers and distributors, acted to censor themselves before Washington jumped in. They set up a common standard of morals and brought in Will Hays to enforce it. Hays was postmaster general at the time, former chairman of the Republican National Committee, and a Presbyterian elder.

In chapter two, we defined *worldly amusements* as having two characteristics: (1) an evil message; and (2) evil methods. Evil ideas and evil means. The evil message presents what is bad as good. Evil methods use wicked actions to communicate the story. The Hays code dealt only with the first problem. Stories no longer glorified gangsters or drinking or sexual promiscuity. Those things were bad. So gangsters and bad girls died in the end. As long as there was a moral, nudity and debauchery could be displayed in a good cause. Cecil B. DeMille became a master at combining religious themes with scenes of debauchery and sex. Will Hays campaigned across America, telling the populace that the movies were moral now. Things settled down but only briefly.

As churches and other moral conservatives caught on to the continued use of evil means, local and state censorship boards sprang up. Offensive scenes were snipped out in some communities. A number of church denominations forbade their members to attend any movie at all. The Hays office published a movie code, endorsed by film producers in March of 1930, which stated in part, "No picture shall be produced that will lower the moral standards of those who see it." The code banned many offensive items in specific terms, but still

Hollywood tried to work around it. In 1934, the Catholic Church set up the Legion of Decency to classify films according to Christian standards. Though Protestant groups supported the legion, many Christians felt that stronger action was needed. Pressed to act, Congress once again considered intervention.

In the middle of the 1930s, everything changed. Fearing government action, Hollywood decided to police itself, strictly censoring its own content in response to public censure. Almost overnight, the movies changed. Nudity was out. Innuendo had to become much more subtle. Both forms of worldliness—evil message and evil means—were censored out by the industry itself. Soon the biggest stars in Hollywood were Shirley Temple and Mickey Rooney, representing perky childhood and robust, but innocent, adolescence. Amazingly, Hollywood entered what is still called its Golden Age. Movies were never better than in the two decades following 1935. Hollywood embraced a sentiment expressed many years later by the great actress Greer Garson, who said of the movies, "I think the mirror should be tilted slightly upward when it's reflecting life . . . not down to the gutter."[16]

So, movies were rescued temporarily in our nation, because of the strong stand of American churches. Christians of all denominations, Protestant and Catholic, held firmly to a standard of decency as old as the Bible itself. The church, determined to be salt and light, resisted the world, and successfully changed the movie industry. The choice, as the church then saw it, was to change the movies or avoid them. Christian leaders did not accept the possibility of accepting Hollywood as it was. God's standard of decency came first.

The Bible was not compromised nor set aside. We owe that generation a big thank you for all the great films of that era—films we can enjoy without embarrassment, films we can enjoy with our children.

Evaluating Christian Responses to the Movies

Real efforts had been made in the twenties and thirties to determine if the movies were a reflection of society or an influence on society. Between 1921 and 1933 the Payne Fund provided $200,000 to the Motion Picture Research Council to study this question. The study was inconclusive, as regards cause and effect, but it determined that some influence was made by the movies on society. Fundamentalists and other church groups found another study done in 1933 to be alarming. The work *Our Movie Made Children* is constantly referred to in the anti- Hollywood literature of the time. The author concluded that "the movies had very harmful effects on children, especially in promoting crime and sexual license.[17]

John R. Rice was the first fundamentalist to write a popular book on the movies. *What is Wrong with the Movies* came out in 1938, not long after the censorship codes were in place. Rice's approach was to blast the movies with invective. His "research," he explained, was based on personal experience that came years before his writing—experience he gained from reading reviews, seeing posters on movie palaces, reading about stars in the paper, "going to the authorities," collecting "reliable" statistics, interviewing others, and not once attending a movie. Rice was unable to discuss any specific film because he had not attended any. Since Rice's contention was that movies are evil, one can respect his choice to keep a distance. After all, one need not see a gladiator show to know it is evil. But in the case of movies, which are quite diverse as individual products, Rice left himself open to a charge of pontificating in ignorance. He concluded that "even an animated cartoon like *Snow White and the Seven Dwarfs* by Walt Disney will do great harm." Rice's rationale went like this:

> They will see advertising runs of other pictures soon to come. Those who attend so-called good pictures will later attend others, just as "moderate drinkers" make drunkards.
>
> The movies are bad. As a class, movie actors and actresses are immoral and are bad company. Movie themes, movies standards of conduct, the motives back of the movie industry are un-Christian and anti-Christian. The proved results of the movies in the lives of multitudes are disastrous and hellish . . . [18]

It is easy to dismiss this rhetorical barrage. It seems unfair. Looking beyond the combative style, we can see his essential argument: people are not discerning.

Remarkably, Rice acknowledged that there are "good pictures." His fear was that Christians will lack discernment in what is good and bad. Being attracted by good pictures would make all pictures worthy of patronage. On this point, Rice has proved to be correct.

Because Rice so thoroughly denounced Hollywood, he never addressed whether or not the church should try to make Christians discerning. Would it be possible to take a less legalistic stand and preserve the integrity of the Christian witness? Instead of answering, Rice offered anecdotes, such as this:

> As one little boy said to his mother after he saw his first moving picture show, "Mother, you just ought to see a picture now and you would never go to prayer meeting anymore!" There is something in the picture show that is the enemy of the prayer meeting, the enemy of the quiet talk with God.[19]

The 1940s saw a big change in the movies. The world had "grown up." More serious themes emerged. Films, such as *Gentlemen's Agreement*, exposed anti-Semitism, and *The Lost Weekend* took viewers into the tragic world of the drunkard. Unfortunately, these thoughtful and tasteful films were condemned as handling immoral subject matter.

A Christian book *Movies and Morals* came out a decade after Rice's book. Herbert Miles, a Baptist pastor in Missouri, used reasoning similar to Rice's but with a less belligerent tone. His work reflected another problem Christians have had in evaluating movies. Miles presented his own statistics by attending numerous films (a step in the right direction) and rating them on a moral category list, which he would check off as he watched.[20] The problem, of course, is that such a survey has no regard for taste or context. If one says *The Lost Weekend* is immoral for showing drinking, does it not count that the *entire* motion picture is designed to show the dangerous, tragic state of the drunkard?

Miles made an excellent point that even in Hollywood's Golden Age, the movies used sin to draw an audience. However, the many movies from that era that did not do this deserve some discussion. Even films that do show some form of evil must be seen in the light of context. At some point, a discussion of the nature of art becomes necessary, but these early Christian movie critics did not address that subject.

Perhaps the most thoughtful work against the movies written in the forties was by Rev. Harry J. Jaeger. I found his article as a tract reprinted from the *Sunday School Times*. Jaeger aimed at the good movies. He attacked the view that high standards should determine Christian viewing habits. He knew that many people in that day found most movies uplifting and that they honored good morals. He fairly outlined five arguments reasonable Christians gave *for* attending the movies. Indeed, these arguments for movies I find very compelling, including one that notes, "Censorship today is of a high moral caliber, eliminating all that might be objectionable." Significantly, this argument for the movies does not exist today, hence the book you are reading.

Jaeger argued that movies are dangerous because they are the product of an *entertainment* industry. The audience, he said, suspends their critical faculties when watching entertainment. They swallow unknowingly the underlying philosophy. What is that philosophy? It is man-centered. The problem with good pictures is that they suggest man is good apart from Christ. He cited as an example the excellent World War II drama *Mrs. Miniver*.

It is harder to bring to Christ a Mrs. Miniver, a person clean and honest and unselfish and contented with life, than it is to convert a crass criminal whose gangsterism both in life and as portrayed on the screen, precludes any claim he might have to worthwhileness. It is difficult to think of any fine, charitable, honest person like Mrs. Miniver as a lost sinner. Such a thought is preposterous to the unregenerate mind! This very confusion is fostered by the screen. The general effect upon millions of moviegoers is to produce in them decisions to be fine like the screen character, in the same way and by the same method. But Christ is excluded; the resultant goodness is pharisaical, the righteousness which in God's holy sight is as "filthy rags."[21]

Jaeger made an interesting point, but should we really object to the world's striving to be clean, honest, unselfish, and contented with life? It is true that Mrs. Miniver does not preach the gospel of grace in the movie, but *Mrs. Miniver* does not deny that gospel either. It is an assumption on Jaeger's part that the character Mrs. Miniver is some kind of humanist. In the film, Mrs. Miniver is a regular churchgoer. The first time she is seen in church, she is in deep prayer. It is certainly possible that she is a fine woman because of her faith. Other scenes point to this as well. The movie's theme music is built around the great hymn *O God Our Help in Ages Past*. When Mrs. Miniver looks from her bedroom window into the sky longing for news of her son, an RAF pilot, the strains of this hymn play in the background. Cinematically, it tells us that in her mind, she is praying. At another point, when Mr. Ballard, the station master, seeks to comfort

her when her husband is absent for five days at Dunkirk, he
quotes the Bible:

> Mr. *Ballard*: Them that goes down to the sea in ships and
> has their business in the great waters, these men see
> the works of the Lord and his wonders in the great
> deep. You can't beat the Bible, can you, when it comes
> to strong feelings?
> Mrs. *Miniver*: No.
> Mr. *Ballard*: No, and no one who throws that over for a
> set of Goebbels and Goerings are gonna win this war.
> That's my comfort, Ma'am.
> Mrs. *Miniver*: Mine, too, Mr. Ballard.

This is a subtle, but clear reference to faith.

Let us suppose Old Hollywood does have a humanistic
bent at times, and I think it *does*. A striving for goodness,
inspired by good films, is a benefit to the gospel, as well as to
the nation. Any aid to moral restraint is good for a society.
And the fact is, people are not able to live up to such a standard, and that makes them aware of their own sin.

I could offer a personal note here. As a young person, I
drew my moral standards from these old films, such as *Mrs.
Miniver*. I had high standards, but I was extremely disappointed that I couldn't live them. My heart was revealed to
me as being sinful because of the morals suggested by the
classic films. A wise Christian would use that "law written
on the heart" to good advantage in presenting the gospel.
The logical extension of Jaeger's view is that we should hope
schools would not teach moral principles because people

might not see their need of Christ. Christians should not fear good morals among unbelievers. When received, good morals make a better world to live in, and they reveal human weakness as well.

Jaeger was also quite unfair in suggesting that this humanistic, godless philosophy underlies all of Hollywood's product. The same man, William Wyler, who gave us *Mrs. Miniver*, also made *Friendly Persuasion*, a delightful and thought-provoking movie about people of faith, who are challenged by the onset of the Civil War. Wyler also made *Ben-Hur*, which presents Christ as God and puts in the mouth of one observing the crucifixion the words, "He has taken the sins of the world upon Himself." A number of films from that era strongly assert the necessity of faith and the reality of Jesus Christ.

Although the 1950s saw more adult themes being handled and a distressing shift in the idea of womanhood, it was the social rebellion of the midsixties that led Hollywood to abandon its censorship code that had been in place for thirty years. Movies started to show visually what previously would have been suggested by dialogue or a facial expression. Nudity and sexual acts were introduced, and soon the ratings system began. Heroes became confused, unsure of themselves, and often broke the law. Since that time, the portrayal of sex and violence has increased. Currently, the sixties-style philosophy has been abandoned in favor of escapist-oriented films, ruled only by a doctrine of political correctness. Scripts get shorter, crashes and explosions bigger. And sex pervades all.

The church was swamped by the radical changes of the sixties. Some churches forbade movie attendance altogether as they always had, now with more reason than ever. Others seem to have just given up and accepted whatever the popular culture had to offer. A unique effort came from Billy Graham's Worldwide Pictures, which tried to enter the secular movie theater with quality films that did, quite deliberately, preach the gospel. These efforts met with some success, most notably the film about Corrie Ten Boom, *The Hiding Place*.

In 1966, *Christianity Today* published an article by J. Melville White suggesting that the church needed to take a new look at Hollywood. The author suggested that young people might actually benefit more by seeing carefully selected films than by seeing none at all. He also suggested that parents and church leaders teach young people how to view movies from a Christian perspective. It was a balanced and well-reasoned approach. The letters it generated from readers demonstrated the sharp split still evident in the evangelical community on the movie question. Many said there should be no compromise. Others, such as Gordon H. Clark of Butler University, strongly denounced a legalism which non-Christians would find senseless.

Where We Are Today

The advice offered by White in 1966 was largely ignored. The gate to the movie palace was cracked open, but no instruction accompanied it. At some point after this time, the gates were flung wide open. Today, the fundamentalist wing of the church still has some elements that forbid the theater altogether. But in the rest of the community of biblical Christians, a lack of appropriate teaching, such as White suggested, has led to an overwhelming tide of acceptance. There are few rules, few comments, very little discussion of moral principle and almost no teaching on amusements. It is almost as if the church has given up on this issue in an increasingly secular age. After two thousand years of moral instruction, desensitization has finally set in.

Prominent evangelicals embrace Hollywood at its most explicit. Josh McDowell, the well-known author on Christian youth, detailed in his book on making right choices that he took his thirteen-year-old daughter to see the shamefully explicit, R-rated movie *Schindler's List*. He used the movie's story of Nazi atrocities to tell his children "there is a truth that is outside me, above our family, and beyond any human—a truth about killing that originates in God."[22] Remarkably, he did not tell his children that the same God has rules about modesty and decency that are equally immutable. Likewise, pop singer Amy Grant sang a title song for a sexually explicit, R-rated Kevin Costner movie. Fuller seminary sponsors film festivals, which include many R-rated, sexually immoral films.

Christian publishers review movies for Christians, with less regard than their secular counterparts for the moral issues of means: language, nudity, and sex. It seems the worst fears of the legalists have come true. John R. Rice warned, "Those who attend so-called good pictures will later attend others just as 'moderate drinkers' make drunkards." The shocking thing is that what sounded like fundamentalist rhetoric back in Hollywood's Golden Age is now reality. It is not even a trend but rather a wholesale capitulation to an immoral industry.

There have been a few voices calling for responsible viewing by believers. Ted Baehr's *Movieguide* and John Evans's *Preview Movie Morality Guide* have made recent attempts at least to inform Christians of content. But few Christians bother with these guides or seek out information. As Ted Baehr has accurately stated, "The overwhelming majority of Christians in the US have the same media habits as the non-Christian population."[23] This statement was based on a major poll conducted in 1983. Why this is so is a big question. The main reason must be that churches are largely silent on the reasons for discernment and the biblical grounds for abstaining from corrupt entertainment.

The Lessons of History

The above has been a brief overview of nearly two thousand years. One thing leaps out of this evidence. What most Christians believe and practice today with regard to worldly amusements is radically different than any other time in church history. The reader needs to know that I did not "cook" the research that appears in this chapter. There may be information that I missed in which church leaders and ministers of the past speak positively about nude women in stage shows, simulated sex acts, and filthy language, deeming them appropriate entertainment. I could not find them. What appears here is a true representation of my research. I looked for any and all references to theatrical amusements. The position of the church, until our time, remained remarkably constant. If anyone is out of step, we are. We must ask what justification we have for our current practices.

Actually, I was surprised that I found so many references to theatrical amusements. Yet upon reflection, this is understandable, since the choices made to attend entertainment and the content of the shows themselves are matters of the soul. Our choices reveal our interests. From the artist's point of view, he has only succeeded when he has touched someone's soul. His joy is in knowing he has touched the heart of his audience in some way. The capacity of the arts to touch the soul has made art's influence a concern for the church, and rightly so. The church is the shepherd of the soul.

One lesson I believe we should learn: ignoring this problem has not helped. Sheep are prone to wander. God's people need to be educated on the subject of amusements from a biblical perspective. The health of the church, the good of souls, and the direction of the culture depend on it. To leave Christians uneducated about this area is foolish. This is the Age of Show Business. The media and entertainment dominate the lives of many, many Christians. It's time we followed those who came before us and say what needs to be said.

In the next chapter, I will discuss the four options open to us as individuals and as churches. There are only four from which to choose.

The Movies: Four Views

I n the last chapter, we quickly covered a lot of material with archaic language and difficult sentence structure. Now I want to simplify the key issues before we go any further. If nothing else, I hope the previous chapter's lesson in church history taught us that this issue of amusements has not been ignored by the church. A brief discussion of the ways in which Christians have responded to the question of theatrical entertainment in general, and the movies in particular, may help us sort out the issues.

Four Views

I see four basic positions a Christian or a church can take on the subject of movies. I will present each view and offer my comments on each as I go. I would encourage you to think through each of these views. You, the reader, will probably find yourself under one of these four headings. Add your own analysis of the strengths and weaknesses of each view. Determine then if you are where you want to be.

AVOIDANCE

The first view is the oldest: *don't go.* Avoidance means an outright ban. Movies are forbidden. Period. Church membership may even require a pledge never to enter a movie theater. This is the response to film that prevailed for the first half of this century. Traditional church instruction regarding attendance of stage plays strongly supports this position. On the surface, it is a simple solution. If there is a problem, stay away.

Arguments in favor of this view:

1. Films make sin glamorous and appealing. In the cinema, the "beautiful people" portray immorality, curse and blaspheme, drink and smoke, etc.
2. The habit of attending movies becomes routine. Most Christians are not discerning and will end up seeing and supporting morally offensive movies. The temptation is too great. It is far safer to simply stay away.
3. Moviegoing is not true recreation; it is escapist. It removes one from reality, leading to a restlessness that seeks other means of escape. The movies are wearying to the soul, not truly restful.
4. Moviegoing sets a bad example for non-Christians. It makes the movie theater seem acceptable, when most of the time it is not. Since unbelievers know that movies generally violate Christian morals, attendance by Christians confirms to the unbeliever that Christians are hypocrites.

Objections to the view:

1. A complete ban on film is legalism, at least when
    presented as church law. Individuals, of course, may
    choose to refrain altogether for conscience' sake. But
    to judge another's spirituality on the form of enter-
    tainment itself is legalistic. There is no scriptural con-
    demnation of attending theatrical amusements or
    movies, per se. Legalism, though it solves the prob-
    lem of having to be discerning, ultimately fails be-
    cause it cannot stand up to reason. It is extremely
    difficult to explain why a movie, such as *Ben-Hur*,
    should not be seen by a follower of Jesus Christ.

2. This view denies the possibility of an art form being
    redeemed by Christ. Is it the form or the content that
    violates Scripture? If it is only the content, cannot
    the form be used to God's glory and to inspire men
    and women to virtue?

3. Non-Christians will probably have a higher level of
    respect for the Christian who exercises individual dis-
    cernment, than they will for the believer who mind-
    lessly follows a church-dictated ban. Does the legal-
    istic approach make the gospel more attractive or less?
    Indeed, it could be argued that legalism presents a
    false understanding of the gospel itself, because it
    denies the liberty which Christ purchased for us.

4. An appreciation of art forms that are not morally of-
    fensive gives the Christian a point of contact with
    unbelievers in their culture. Many films can be used
    as a tool for discussion about spiritual issues. If high

standards are adopted, this too, bears witness that moral principle is more important than amusement.

5. If I may add an argument from experience, my own background with the movies does not allow me to adopt the legalistic approach, as tempting as it may be. When I was young, the classic movies of Old Hollywood had a profound impact on me for good. They helped shape my moral values and gave me a standard of conduct for which to aim. Many films portrayed a respectful attitude toward women, which helped me. A rather silly movie called *Counterpoint* ended my love of rock music by exposing me to the symphonies of Beethoven. Old films taught me about honor, loyalty, integrity, patriotism, respect for women, and self-sacrifice. I found the movies a source for good in my life.

SILENCE

This view is the easiest: *don't talk about it*. Ministers should address other topics but not this one. Let people see what they want, when they want. Christians shouldn't bother themselves with an issue such as this; it might upset someone. Churches shouldn't talk about it because it is not "seeker friendly." It is more acceptable to discuss the sins of others than to confront our own moral issues.

Arguments in favor of this view:

1. There are none. This view has nothing to commend it. I know of no Christian who actively defends this view, but it is the de facto view of churches and Christian leaders who refuse to confront the issue.

Objections to this view:

1. This is a failure of leadership. To leave the flock unaware of the dangers of immoral entertainment is
   cowardly and negligent. A man of God cannot lament fornication, out-of-wedlock births, pornographic addictions, and a basic cultural slide, without confronting one of the principal causes of these
   evils.
2. This view fails intellectually as well. It falsely assumes
   that art has no power and therefore isn't important
   enough to discuss.

ENGAGEMENT

The third view says that Christians should be engaged with
the culture. We should immerse ourselves in the experience of
those around us, as long as we exercise reasonable caution that
we not be too overcome by it. One might call this the "artistic
standards" view. As long as the work is good artistically, it
doesn't matter what the specific content is. Filthy language,
nudity, people simulating sex acts—at some level, all of this is
acceptable if it serves some higher purpose. This is, relatively
speaking, a very new view among Christian leaders, but it has
dominated the church for about twenty years now.

I understand this view. I held it myself for several years
during my college days. Although I was offended by the immoral or vulgar elements in films, I chose to look for a higher
good. In practical terms, this was a very easy way to live. It
seemed sophisticated, and let me see pretty much what I
wanted to see.

A typical example of this view can be found in a glowing review given to *Rob Roy* by Pamela C. Johnson in an April 1995 edition of *World* magazine. The R-rated movie, she explains, includes "explicit scenes of sexual violence and torture." But for her, the "point of view" redeems the film. Johnson writes,

> Some Christians will disagree, but I believe that the mark of a good film is not whether it details or tries to ignore the depravity of man, but within what context man's depravity is explored. Watching *Rob Roy*, the audience rightly cringes at cruelty and weeps with the defenseless.

Arguments in favor of this view:

1. This view stands firmly against legalism. It affirms an individual's liberty to practice his faith in his own way.
2. This view recognizes the importance of art. Such a view allows the Christian to interact with the world on its own terms. Francis Schaeffer exemplified this approach in his work. He could look at a film like Antonioni's *Blow Up* and see past the prurient sexual content to examine it philosophically. He used the common experience of such films as a platform for discussion with unbelievers.

Objections to this view:

1. It's against the Bible. Pamela Johnson's comment that whether a film is good or not has nothing to do with how it "details . . . the depravity of man" is merely

her opinion. The apostle Paul's moral doctrine says, "it is disgraceful even to speak of the things which are done by them in secret" (Eph. 5:12). If it is shameful to discuss the details of depravity, how much more offensive to decency must it be to pay people to act out such "details" for our amusement! No matter how sophisticated one wishes to be, the Scripture is still the authority. The Christian's moral conscience owes its allegiance to God's Word, not to its own flawed moral compass. The Scripture must inform our choices and tastes.

2. It is against the law of love. This view demonstrates a profound lack of consideration for the spiritual well-being of the performers in these immoral films. The violation of their modesty alone should make Christians recoil at participation in such amusements. It is impossible to imagine Jesus giving approval for the use of actors in this way.

3. It denies the power of art. This view would claim to have the most respect for the arts, but in truth, it suggests that the immoral content of these films has no effect on the soul. The belief that such displays of sensual corruption for entertainment do not harm the soul directly opposes the teaching of the church from the beginning to the present time. The idea that such entertainment is acceptable is entirely new, and yet the fruit of this new idea has not been increased purity—not by any measure. It has not furthered the cause of Christ for Christians to have shared in worldly and carnal knowledge through film.

HIGH STANDARDS

This final view suggests that Christians should hold the arts to a clear standard of morality in order to justify Christian patronage. Rather than giving us the details of depraved acts, good art can reveal the depraved heart through well-written stories, enlightening us to the evil we may find within ourselves. We learn nothing by being made aware of the details of sexual acts or rape. We do learn by seeing the ruinous effects of pride, bitterness, anger, and yes, even lusts, which can be shown without the lurid details. For example, Old Hollywood made a very moving story called *Johnny Belinda* about a sexual assault on a mute girl. Unlike modern films, which frequently detail depravity, the assault was never shown. It didn't need to be. The audience grieved the wickedness of the act, just knowing it had taken place.

Arguments in favor of this view:

1. It avoids legalism. The legalist seeks to go beyond Scripture. The high-standards view seeks to apply Scripture accurately, without adding to it or detracting from it.

2. It gives art its due. The high-standards view recognizes art's power, both for good and evil. It does not condemn cinema as an inherently irredeemable art form but recognizes the potential danger of its powerful effect on our souls.

3. This view honors the performers. The most neglected—and perhaps the most important—moral dimension of the high-standards view is its concern for the actors, who are often turned into little more than

harlots for the screen. It is typical of our age that we don't consider how we use other people to satisfy our lusts or our moral laziness. We just don't care enough.

4. It honors the Word of God. Scripture does speak to these issues. We do have a responsibility for what we put before our eyes, feed into our hearts, and spend God's money on.

Objections to this view:

1. Different Christians may be at different places in their conscience. Defining entertainment standards for them, instead of letting them grow to a godly position themselves, may be divisive and create tension among brothers. There is a danger of a holier-than-thou attitude.

2. It is difficult to sustain a high-standards approach. Moral instruction in entertainment and the arts will have to be an ongoing ministry of every church for this to work. Each generation will need guidance in this area. Every Christian will need to be reminded not to love the world.

Thoughts on the Four Views

The reader will strongly suspect that I favor view four. I do. Strongly. It is not that I disdain all the other views, or have not considered them. Only the silence view do I disdain, because it is indefensible. As I mentioned, I once held to the "engagement" theory. I was a film student. I believed in the significance of the art form. I was very influenced by the

writings of Francis Schaeffer at that time in my life as well.
And while I still appreciate much about Dr. Schaeffer, I believe he was wrong to ignore the dangers of popular art forms,
not for their ideas alone but for their very content. I also believe he demonstrated a remarkable disregard for the moral
health of the performers in such amusements.

There are two objections to the high-standards view: one
from the engagement point of view, the other from the avoidance camp. I will try to address them.

The first objection to the high-standards view is important, because no one wants to see believers divided over the
issue of what movies people see, nor should an attitude of
pride swell the heads of those who have chosen high standards. The danger of developing an attitude of moral superi-
ority is not limited to entertainment. Any affirmation of high,
moral standards can lead to this attitude. The solution is not
to forsake biblical standards or to hide them, but for leaders
to resist this arrogant spirit and to teach against it.

In the church I pastor, people obviously have had to confront the entertainment question. While my flock has been
careful to hear what I have to say on the matter, not everyone has changed their behavior. I don't label as being "weak"
and "unfit for service" those people whose view differs from
mine. I do pray for their understanding, and I preach with
conviction the standard I believe the Bible teaches. Beyond
that, we accept each other in Christ. The leaders set the tone
of acceptance, but they also live and teach God's standard.

The second objection listed against the high-standards
view would most likely come from the legalist. I sympathize.
It is easier just to forbid theatrical amusements. The avoidance view is attractive because we are so weak. People al-

lowed to attend any movies, even virtuous films, may well become indiscriminate viewers. Most programs for recovering addicts of one kind or another have to make lots of rules. Sometimes rules are necessary for the weak. Still, my very being resists the legalist approach to the Christian life.

It *is* a chore to systematically preach against the culture, but we have to do it. The church has faithfully done it for two thousand years. Banning film is easier, but it's not right. We must teach our people to be discerning. We have to teach them not to go to the movies casually. They must learn the biblical standards. We have to teach them to find out about a movie's content in advance. This takes effort. It takes self-control. It takes work. But the payoff is worth it. I received the following letter from one of our high-school girls after I preached two sermons on immoral entertainment, using the movie *Titanic* as a springboard.

> I wanted to let you know you did a wonderful job preaching these last two Sundays. Your love and concern for the body of Christ is truly seen through your words.
>
> A few months ago, I made strong standards about the things that I would watch. I cannot remember the last time I went to the movie theater, and I do not desire to watch things that are unpleasing to God. Your sermon helped me to realize that my convictions will pay off now and in the end. I want others to see me as a godly woman in all areas of my life.

These convictions grew out of an understanding of the Bible's high standards. They were not forced through legalism. I believe the behaviors resulting from true conviction will be more enduring than those imposed by church rules.

In this case, I believe the harder road of moral teaching will produce greater convictions in our people. The Holy Spirit is alive and able to instruct His own. The difficult road of character development requires mutual change and growth of church leaders and members as fellow human beings, subject to the same temptations and moral dilemmas. I myself still feel the pull of the world. I love movies. It hasn't always been easy to live as one who holds the high standards view. There have been a few films I really wanted to see, but did not. Kenneth Branaugh's *Hamlet* comes to mind. I knew from the preview that this film was immodest and used evil means. Why Branaugh worked a sex scene into Hamlet I will never understand, and how he did it I don't need to know. Part of me missed the experience some of my friends savored. Part of me felt joy in choosing against my desires. In the end, it is only a movie, and my life was not diminished for having missed something that is a moral offense to our great God. And maybe, just maybe, if enough Christians stay away, Hollywood will consider that it is not wise to force offensive elements into otherwise worthy entertainment.

Chapter Five

What is Good Art?

If there is any aspect of human nature that proves beyond question that man is not an animal, it would be his creativity. The aesthetic sense—the creation and appreciation of beauty—is unique to man among the creatures of the earth. The birds may sing the songs nature gives to them, but man writes the songs he sings. In countless ways, people experience, interpret, and communicate about life through art. No animal does this. Perhaps evolution's greatest enemy is a painting or a symphony. The aesthetic sense can best, perhaps only, be accounted for by man's being made in God's image. Looking at Genesis, Dorothy Sayers suggests that all we have learned about God, leading up to the declaration that man is made in His image, is that God is the Creator.[1] Scripture plainly intends that we see our creativity as a mark of the divine image.

In life we find humans are creative beings. The Bible tells us why. The existence of art, then, is at once validated by and supportive of Christian theology.

The creation and enjoyment of art is a supremely human thing. It is, in itself, a divine gift, a genuine blessing, bound up in us. That is why even very decadent cultures express themselves artistically. The presence of depravity does not remove this human capacity to be creative. The sin of man merely bends this capacity to serve his depravity. This fact is extremely important to any discussion of art from a Christian perspective. The existence of art is not the sign of moral strength, but it is the sign of the divine image. It marks our humanness. Still, man is fallen. His fallen condition is often expressed in his art.

When we say that art is *good*, what do we mean? We may mean that it manifests great skill. Or we may appreciate the way an artist expresses his experience or point of view. Usually we mean that it has touched us. In some way we have been "held" by the artist's work. For the true artist, this is one of his greatest pleasures—to see his work draw the interest and attention of another. It need not be weighty and ponderous to be good art. As Harold Gardiner writes:

> We can be held by pure fun; we can be held by stark tragedy: James Thurber and E.B. White are, in this respect, no less master craftsmen than Dostoevski and Shakespeare.[2]

When I was in high school, my friend Scott Stallard and I labored for a year to produce, on Super-8 film, a ninety-minute, musical-comedy version of *Macbeth*, which we wrote, directed and edited ourselves. The task was daunting, to say the least. The musical numbers were especially difficult with the primitive equipment we had. We rewrote the lyrics to great-American show tunes and fit them to Shakespeare's tale of woe. Lady Macbeth sang "Can't Help Lovin' that Thane of Mine" to Jerome Kern's *Showboat* tune. King Duncan praised son Malcolm with a medieval version of Cole Porter's "You're the Top."

At last came the great unveiling—the premiere. We got permission to use the basement hall of the Lutheran church I attended while growing up, and we had an audience of about fifty people, namely friends and family members of our dozen or so cast members. Scott and I were ridden with anxiety, realizing this was a real audience. It was our task to amuse them for the evening. There was nothing else on the bill. Since the film was a broad comedy, it would be clear within minutes whether we had succeeded or had wasted the audience's evening and a year of our lives.

As the film slowly made its way through the projector, the laughter came. We were elated. It was one of the most remarkable moments of sheer joy in my life. People laughed, stamped their feet, giggled—usually at the right things. Not every idea worked, but we "held" them. As creators of this little show, we had succeeded. And that was everything. I had been in plays before and had heard applause, but the joy of this experience was heightened because it was my work. I had a hand in every second of the film. No one would label our work "good art," but we did share the experience of an artist's pleasure.

Film as Art

Film is an art form. A good film, like a good painting or musical composition, holds an audience. Indeed, film is a unique blend of many creative arts. It is most like the theater, but it differs even from that in its ability to create diverse images; the "close-up" is one unique example. Film also differs from theater in its incredible capacity to control time through cutting. These cinematic elements, along with the skills of actors, composers, designers, etc., combine in an effort to touch an audience—to hold them. We say it is a good film if it held us, and a bad film if it didn't. Cost and complexity are not the only factors in a film's success. A huge budget and a cast of thousands may bore us to tears, while a shoestring budget and two actors may grip us for two hours.

More sophisticated viewers contemplate how deeply they were held. Often a movie can hold one's attention, but doesn't leave one with anything. The feeling is that two hours have been wasted. The viewer may have the sense of being manipulated emotionally rather than having genuinely encountered that which is real or human. Some filmmakers know exactly how to make an audience cry, but they achieve this by sheer technique.

The enormously popular but dreadful movie, *Independence Day,* is a good example of shallow audience manipulation. Buttons are pressed for romance, laughter, grief, effects-based exhilaration, more laughter, patriotism, and victory. None of it connects to anything but shallow sentiment. None of the people are real. The emotions are formulaic, not genuine. When someone is supposed to die, soft music and scenes of grieving children bring the audience to tears. It matters not that the death is immediately forgotten by the characters in the movie. They have switched to a new mood without growth or meaning. But it works. People adore such films.

The art form has that kind of power to manipulate and please the undiscriminating viewer.

The Moral Imperative

What do we mean by *good art*? Is it only its ability to "hold" us? What about *good* in the moral sense? Does the artist have any obligation to the moral law of God? Is it legitimate for him to use his skill for depraved purposes? And if he serves evil, can his work be considered good? Should the artist's freedom to create give him license to teach evil or use human beings shamefully?

We have said that art is a channel of human expression. Certainly then, for Christians, our words, even our thoughts, come under the authority of God. Human beings are judged for their expression (see Matt. 12:36–37). We may not use God's name in vain, slander our brother, bear false testimony, or even call someone a fool, with the intent to diminish him. But it is just as much a sin to be "speaking arrogant words of vanity" used "to entice [people] by fleshly desires . . ." (2 Pet. 2:18). We are accountable to God, and the label of "art" on human expression does not remove this accountability in the slightest way. What, then, are the moral imperatives of art?

The moral measure of art is truth. Frank Gabelein, in his wonderful book *The Christian, the Arts, and the Truth*, defined *art* as "the expression of truth through beauty." By *beauty* he did not mean "something pretty," but rather "something with aesthetic value." The artist is bound by truth. He has an obligation to truth. The Christian is bound to the concept of absolute truth, or that which reflects the truth of God and His moral order. Modern artists who build their work on a

notion of relative truth fail because they have missed seeing
the world as it really is. As Dr. Gabelein put it:

> Art that distorts the truth is no more pleasing to God
> than any other kind of untruth. Surely it is not too much
> to say that the God of all truth looks for integrity in artis-
> tic expression as well as in theology.[3]

Film, as any other work of art, should be judged on the
criterion of truth. Now, truth has varying applications, according to the kind of work being examined. What we are talking
about is not sheer factual information. It is understood that
drama "fills in the gaps" of history, for example. Often fiction
has no factual basis. It may involve that which is unreal, such
as science fiction or fantasy. Truth, in these genres of fiction,
has to do with point of view, not point of fact.

Let's look at some of the ways we should consider truth as
it applies to the art of film. We can begin with the factual.

True to Historical Reality

Representations of actual events in drama or literature
have a certain obligation to truth. It is assumed by the audience that some things are not known and that the "holes"
must be filled with made-up dialogue. Even characters are
sometimes invented to bring coherence. But the audience
also expects that this dramatic license will not violate essential truths. The fine 1989 film *Glory* managed to capture both
the spirit and many of the details of the all-Black, Fifty-fourth
Massachusetts regiment's rise to fame during the Civil War.

Were some details altered? Yes. Fiction filled in the gaps, but the story was told truly.

Contrast *Glory* with 1997's *Titanic*, a film that manipulated history into an unrecognizable smear against western civilization and against the wealthy. If ever one wanted to condemn the rich, the story of the RMS *Titanic* would be one to stay away from—unless the artist is arrogant enough to radically rewrite history. Director James Cameron is just such an artist. Profoundly untrue to the event and the people involved, *Titanic* substituted simplistic villainy for often-noble humanity. One of many examples is that of poor First Officer William Murdoch, a man who stayed at his post until the end and gave his life selflessly aiding others. Cameron portrays him as a cold-hearted huckster, taking bribes from rich people in exchange for getting them seats on lifeboats. The evidence for such evil? None. It never happened.

It seems obvious that Cameron was on a mission to trash the values of Edwardian civilization—our past; that is all. Of course, Murdoch's family and hometown of Dalbeattie, Scotland, were quite upset with this worldwide slander. Twentieth Century Fox took eight thousand dollars from its multibillion-dollar profits to erect a memorial in Dalbeattie, celebrating Murdoch's heroism. One wonders what percentage of those who see *Titanic* will see the memorial.

In spite of its blatant disregard for true history, *Titanic* was named "Best Picture of the Year" by the Motion Picture Academy of Arts and Sciences. Good art? Not if we accept Harold Gardiner's words that "art is not the dramatic embodiment of a lie."[4] Historical truth should be preserved by the theater. Remarkably, James Cameron openly acknowledged film's power to shape reality in people's minds. "We have a great responsibility," he told *Newsweek*. "Whatever we make will become the truth, the visual reality that a generation will accept."[5]

Similarly, the Russian revolutionary leader Lenin loved the cinema for its power to rewrite history for a mass audience. The state could disseminate its own truth. In our Media Age, a time when books are seldom read, movies define historical truth. Films, such as *Titanic, Gandhi, Dances with Wolves*, and many others, blatantly rewrite whole eras, usually with an intent to create resentment against Western culture. They succeed because people simply don't know any better. Most people go to the movies to be entertained. Ignorant of true history, and in no mood for critical analysis, they are ripe for propagandizing. These films, in their own way, are just as much a lie as *Birth of a Nation* was when it celebrated the derring-do of the Ku Klux Klan back in 1915.

True to Our Humanity

The French philosopher Pascal, a Christian, defines a key function of true religion:

> The greatness and wretchedness of man are so evident that the true religion must necessarily teach us both that there is in man some great source of greatness and a great source of wretchedness. [6]

Many philosophies and religions fail this crucial reality test. In this quotation, substitute for the words "the true religion," the words "true art," and you will have, I believe, an equally challenging statement. Art must tell the truth about man: that he is above the animals and endowed with significance and dignity, and also that he is weak and touched by sin.

Christians should expect drama to present man as a sinner in need of grace. We should also expect art to present man as a moral agent before God—responsible for his actions, capable of noble action as well as foolishness. This understanding is what gives ancient literature its enduring greatness. Homer's heroes, for example, were fully human by this definition. Good art will have a correct understanding of man as a foundation for whatever individual stories are told.

When one thinks of the great films, there is complexity in the characters. Whether it is Humphrey Bogart's wounded heart in *Casablanca* or John Wayne's bitter spirit in *The Searchers*, real human traits are expressed by their characters. They are not two-dimensional, cartoon heroes or villains. They are men. Bogart's Rick is representative of many American strengths. He is unimpressed by power or social position. He's clever and yet capable of compassion. He roots for the underdog. When his loneliness and desire leave him vulnerable to sin, however, Rick finds his personal desires in serious conflict with the higher good. One strongly suspects that if his true love's husband, Victor Lazlo, had not been a great man, Rick may have chosen to steal his wife.

Ethan Edwards, the bitter character in John Ford's classic western *The Searchers*, is the kind of individual who loves and hates intensely. He has made bad choices and has lost his place in society. His whole life is a struggle between his wild nature and his attachments to civilization, represented by family. He is always pushing away those who love him the most. When his brother's family is murdered in an Indian raid and his niece is kidnapped, he relentlessly pursues the criminals and the last of his family. The years pass, and his search for his niece turns into a hunt as he realizes she will have been acclimated to Indian culture, probably even married. He decides to kill her instead of save her. His young companion, Martin, is the voice of conscience. Even when he does the right thing, in the end, Ethan is alone. He found kindness, but not closeness.

A Christian does not demand that drama ignore the reality of sin. Indeed, a cinematic world where all is sweetness and light would be not only poor art, but also a lie. Yet the need to be true to the human condition should not be misconstrued as an invitation to display sin in all of its offensive details. Blatant exhibition of sin pushes beyond commentary on the fallen human condition and into further degradation, becoming part of humanity's problem instead of something from which we may benefit. Additionally, art cannot be considered successful if it has taken a stance against the Creator and Judge of all who live. This leads to the next point.

True to the Moral Order

Right and wrong are clearly delineated in God's book, the Bible. Scripture is, in part, the revelation of a moral law that is binding on all people at all times. The Bible tells us that all men have the "law written on their hearts." But it also tells us that men are under God's wrath because they "suppress the truth in unrighteousness."[7] They reject the law. They cast aside the standard. This is evil.

An artist, in expressing his understanding of the world, succeeds or fails, in part, owing to how well his point of view corresponds to his Creator's. *Gone with the Wind*, for example, allows us to see that Scarlett is beautiful and Rhett is a charming rogue, but it also plainly reveals the inadequacy of these qualities to create a good life. To be certain we understand their failure, the story gives us Melanie's character as a contrast. Some have criticized Melanie's lack of glamour or feminine allure. Physically weak, mild-mannered, and plain—when compared to Scarlett—Melanie's only real strength is an unfailing kindness born of faith. She is no less interesting than Scarlett by film's end, for of all the characters, she alone knows what love really is. Her radiance increases as her love is tried, while Scarlett's beauty is marred by drink and bitterness.

There is a moral core in *Gone with the Wind* consistent with the Bible's moral teaching. For the Christian, this is an important part of the "good" when we say *Gone with the Wind* is a good film. A film does not need to be "preachy" to be good, but any art that deals with moral beings must have a moral center based on the truth of God's moral framework. When the world calls *Gone with the Wind* "good," it is not referring to this moral center.

In 1998, when the American Film Institute chose the best 100 American movies in the industry's first 100 years, it made its selections on other-than-moral grounds. On the list, only a few notches below *Gone with the Wind*, was *The Graduate* (1967), a film some found far more preachy than *Gone with the Wind*. A true product of the sixties, this dark comedy decried materialism, hypocrisy, conformity, etc., but it did so from a philosophical perspective that was rebellious, and little else. Rejection of the status quo was not based on a discovery of its failure to conform to the moral order. Rather, it was simply overthrown by a smug, in-your-face youth culture. That same youth culture grew up to be just as materialistic and phony as the world it criticized.

With its lack of moral focus, *The Graduate* fits right in with other critically acclaimed films from the late sixties. As Neil Hurley says of such films:

> Many of these films have a subtle Manichaean taint to them; they do not take seriously a world that is imperfect and unfinished, satisfying themselves that the mere opposition to this world is equivalent to achieving the perfection and harmony it lacks.[8]

The Graduate was popular with that generation, but in today's sentimental environment, it seems archaic. The "provocative" and "shocking" sexual material of yesterday is exceeded by network television shows of today. Lacking current shock value, and based on a shallow philosophy of mere opposition to the culture, the film doesn't hold up. It is dated because it fails to embrace lasting truths.

Of course, by God's standard, *The Graduate* has serious moral problems of method as well as message. Its teasing, visual sexuality and "coarse jesting" are in themselves a violation of the moral order revealed in Scripture. This puts the film squarely in the category of moral evil, which leads us to the next area of truth.

True to the Audience

It is the moral duty of the artist to realize that he is communicating with human beings. There is so much more at issue than holding the audience's attention. The audience is made up of moral beings, many easily swayed by the power of art. There is much more to a successful film than interesting camera work, witty dialogue, talented acting, and all the rest that has to do with craft. There is also its influence on people.

I will not try to argue that films influence people. It has been evident for many years in speech, fashion, manners, and even employment. All writers on cinema, whose work is worthy of attention, recognize the power of the medium to influence people. Most argue that the influence is subtle, even unconscious. Incrementally, attitudes are altered, beliefs are shifted, and desires are redirected as an individual is repeatedly exposed to Hollywood's understanding of the world. This power to influence is multiplied for the average film goer, because most people go to the movies to have a good time. The critical faculties are turned off.

When is art true to its audience? As Harold Gardiner explains, art must "appeal to man *as man*, not merely to man as an animal."[9] His point is that man is more than mere pleasures and passions. Each of us is a rational soul, and our reason should govern our passions. Art can appeal to the pleasures and passions of man, apart from his moral judgement, but this is wrong. Art can feed his lusts, feed his hatred of certain groups, make crime heroic, etc. Art can bend its powers to serve these passions, but this would make it poor art, because it would be an assault on the viewer's humanity, which is so much more than these passions.

This kind of poor art is exactly what people mean when they describe certain works or entertainment as "debased." Gardiner gives an excellent example:

> Let us suppose a man writes a book in which his clear and explicit purpose is to arouse racial hatred. He is out, we suppose, to prove that Negroes or Asians are degenerates and utterly subhuman. He does this in the most exquisite prose, in the most superbly structured narrative, through characters most incisively conceived and described— would his novel be a work of art? No—for the simple reason that he is appealing to emotions that are unworthy, inhuman, unrecognizable as the emotions of the generality of mankind.[10]

Gardiner's evaluation is exactly right. Art which promotes, encourages, or delights in evil is unworthy of appreciation. Art does not exist in a vacuum. It is part of the world of people. It is meant to touch people. It influences people. That very influence is under the watchful eye of the Judge of all the earth. He not only sees the effect on behavior, He also sees the effect on thinking and feeling. He even sees the motive of the artist—writer, director, producer, or performer.

Applying the Tests of Truth

Let us return to Gone with the Wind once more as a case study. We can apply these tests of truth to this beloved American classic to determine if it holds up as art. We don't need to argue about the cinematic craftsmanship as applied to Gone with the Wind; it is universally recognized as a very good, perhaps great, film. Not a few would call it a masterpiece.

IS IT TRUE TO HISTORICAL REALITY?

Gone with the Wind is fiction, but it is set in the era surrounding the American Civil War. It takes place in the South and is a reasonably accurate representation of events of that time. If *Gone with the Wind* could be faulted, it would be on the issue of race and slavery. Here the record is mixed. The movie suggests that the prewar South was a rather idyllic world. There is slavery, but the Wilkes and the O'Haras are kind to their slaves (as some southerners were). Ashley Wilkes even tells Scarlett he plans to free his slaves if the war doesn't do it. We never see the darker side of that "peculiar institution." Scarlett's slaves are even seen merrily going off to "dig for the South." Their apparent desire to keep out the Yankees and preserve their world seems most unlikely.

There are some racial stereotypes in *Gone with the Wind*, but there is depth to the Black characters that diminishes any offense, even by modern standards. Butterfly McQueen's character, Prissy, is called a "simple-minded darkie" by Rhett, but that's what she is. He does not say that all Blacks are simple minded. We are shocked when Scarlett strikes Prissy in the face, but later Scarlett slaps her own sister the same way. (Butterfly McQueen has said she would have slapped Prissy too.)

Prissy's character is offset by Scarlett's Mammy, a role that won Hattie McDaniel an Oscar. Her battle to keep Scarlett decent provides some moments of real humor, and she comes across as a woman of dignity. Rhett says that she is one of the few people whose respect he would like to have. *Gone with the Wind* does not deserve the label of "racist," because it affirms the humanity and uniqueness of its characters.

Reconstruction, however, is presented in a way that leans toward the portrayal in *Birth of a Nation*, but with much more subtlety. We see proud Blacks flaunting their new positions of power, Yankees manipulating freed slaves for votes, and the unfair burdens placed on the former ruling class. We don't see anything good about Blacks being granted their freedom. There's a genuine nostalgia for the well-ordered world of the prewar South. In that, the film is flawed. Modern movies are so politically correct on these issues that they become painfully predictable, but *Gone with the Wind* errs the other way. Its omissions are too significant.

Is It True to Our Humanity?

Scarlett and Rhett are very attractive people who find happiness elusive. Scarlett is profoundly self-centered, even in her misplaced devotion to Ashley Wilkes. She is strong, but hard. As Rhett tells her: "You are no lady." She knows how to get what she wants, but she wants the wrong things. Rhett is self-reliant, worldly-wise, and brave, but he doesn't know how to love. His pride and worldliness do not allow him much room for forgiveness. His charm and wit become barriers to affection when he feels slighted. Both of these characters know Melanie Wilkes, the true Christian, whose behavior embodies the Sermon on the Mount. Scarlett and Rhett's refusal to learn from Melanie's wisdom and example causes much misery and eventually destroys their marriage.

In short, these characters are not all good or all bad. Like most of us, they have mixed qualities. What they are, in biblical terms, is *lost*. And the film acknowledges this lostness. We do not need to read it into the story. We admire Scarlett's strength, but we are horrified at her cruelty and heartlessn-ess. Her decision to "never be hungry again" no matter what it takes, destroys her soul. It is Scarlett whom the film wisely labels a hypocrite. At the same time, Melanie's death has a redemptive effect on Scarlett. Her eyes are opened; she finds hope. *Gone with the Wind* is true to our humanity because its characters ring true. They have greatness and wretchedness, and that greatness and wretchedness are defined by a stan-dard consistent with God's law.

IS IT TRUE TO THE MORAL ORDER?

Gone with the Wind does maintain the moral "point of view." It takes positions on people's failures. Rhett Butler is a deeply flawed human being. He drinks, smokes, frequents prostitutes, and lives on the margins of the law. And he is charming. Some sinners are charming. Is this depiction a violation of the moral order? No. The film will not leave us with Rhett as just a charm-ing rogue. Change reveals the complexity of the man. He de-clares he will never risk his life for the South, only for profit. Living only for himself, later he sees his own weakness com-pared with men of honor. On a road full of walking wounded, Scarlett tells Rhett that he should be proud he was smart enough to stay out of the war. "I'm not so proud," he says. When the cause is lost, he joins up. He has a conscience. It seems he wants to change. He desires to marry Scarlett, whereas earlier he was "not a marrying man."

But Rhett's weaknesses catch up with him. Because he has no spiritual center to his life, the death of his child nearly drives him insane. Only Melanie can bring him back from madness. He is unable to make his marriage work. His pride keeps him from working with Scarlett's weaknesses. When things go bad, divorce is all he can come up with. He chooses the easy way, as he has all his life.

Melanie, of course, is the film's moral conscience. Her position as the moral example is critical to the story. She loves her enemies. She thinks the best of everyone. She is herself virtuous, but she is kind even to Belle, the prostitute. Without Melanie, Gone with the Wind would sink into a morally confused melodrama. Her presence gives the film a deliberately moral point of view—a missing ingredient in so many films since the 1960s.

Is It True to the Audience?

Gone with the Wind has the moral center, but does it fail the morals of its audience? It does not. The film certainly has opportunities to trip up the viewer's own morality with tantalizing images of sin. It does not do it. Even Rhett's sins are not portrayed in offensive detail. When we see him in the brothel, he hasn't so much as untied his tie. Even the wicked ladies are well covered. It is remarkable how little one has to see to know what's been going on.

Is Gone with the Wind good art? Yes. Could it be better? Yes. It was weak on the truth test of history, but not fatally. It is a human drama with a strong moral center. It respects God's law and the audience. It has earned the right to Christian patronage.

Putting Back the Missing Dimension

In evaluating the worth of their entertainment choices, Christians must learn to consider the moral quality of a film as being as important as its craftsmanship. Secular critics will not do this. Even Christian reviewers are inconsistent, picking out some moral purpose—usually, that love is more important than money—as a justification to call a film "good," ignoring elements that are, in fact, morally debilitating. This is a big mistake. It is not too much to ask that films not promote evil in any way. Many good films—some of which made the AFI's 100 best-movie list—follow the moral order right down the line, yet remain works of great power. They respect their audience's humanity. They agree that some things must be handled with sensitivity so as not to offend or hurt people.

When I say these films follow the moral order right down the line, I mean that they do not violate decency and that they consistently hold the moral point of view. The characters may be sinners and remain sinners, but the tone, purpose, and drift of the whole work supports the moral order. It is not necessary for Rick in *Casablanca*, for example, to become a Christian, renounce drinking and smoking, and become a missionary to North Africa. That is not what the film is about. The film is about people needing to sacrifice for the cause against Hitler. It is really a tract to persuade Americans to get involved in World War II. Rick represents America, torn between what is right and the desire for peace and pleasure. The fact is, Rick concludes, "The problems of three little people don't amount to a hill of beans in this crazy world." That is, there is a higher good than my personal desires. I am content with that lesson in that film. Rick's failings are not detailed. His virtues are. That carries the audience to the side of virtue, while recognizing genuine weakness.

Remember, Christian, God is the governor of the universe. All human activity, including the artistic, is under His moral authority. Can a Christian really label "good" anything that flaunts itself in the face of that moral authority? Art cannot be divorced from what is true before God. When artists make such a separation, they are in sin. When we embrace their sin, we stand against His rule as well.

Of all the arts, drama—stage or film—requires the highest degree of moral analysis. Drama is about human life, and because it touches people, it changes them. Obviously, a painting of a bowl of fruit or of a building needs little moral scrutiny. In this way, of course, art should be free to merely express our enjoyment of beauty without an obviously "religious" purpose. It is an honor to God that our humanity is creative and expresses itself creatively.

Art that touches the soul, however, needs justification. That is, artists are accountable for what they do and how they do it. Christians are accountable to "abstain from every form of evil"[11]. Some Christians suggest we are not to judge unbelievers. God alone judges. We cannot criticize them for failing to produce works with a moral center they do not possess. There is much truth in this. The issue of moral discretion, then, is not so much left with the artist as with the Christian patron. The accountability falls upon us to "not participate in the unfruitful deeds of darkness." We are not judging the artist by not supporting his work; we are rightly judging ourselves and our duty. Christian duty does not end at the ticket counter of a movie theater and pick up again when the exit sign is passed. Being separated from sin and not loving the world must include the arts as well. Our love of culture must never be exalted over our love of God.

Chapter Six

What Does the Bible Say?

I t should be clear from chapter four that I support the high-standards view of entertainment. Movies, television, and the arts must earn my attention and involvement by fully respecting my moral standards. I won't go to the movies just because they are there. I won't go just because we always go on Friday night and "there's nothing else to do." As in all areas of life, the standard must rule. I conform to it, not tweak it around to match my moods or desires. The movies, especially in these times, are off limits unless I am confident my moral standards will not be compromised. The question now is this: Where do I find these standards? There is only one answer to that question: What does God say?

The Need for Standards Outside of Us

First of all, the Bible says we are prone to deception. In life we are wary of deceivers: politicians, car salespeople, infomercials, etc., but we often fail to examine what the Bible calls the most deceitful thing in the world:

> The heart is more deceitful than all else, and is desperately sick; who can understand it? (Jer. 17:9)

More than anyone else, we fool ourselves. Because this is true, I once did a study on deception. Finding each place in the New Testament where it said, "Do not be deceived," I sought to identify and explain just what it is we're not supposed to be deceived about. My assumption being, if the Bible says "Do not be deceived" about a certain area, then that area must be one in which people are particularly prone to deception. One of these texts on deception relates directly to the entertainment issue. What follows is from Ephesians 5:3–7:

> But do not let immorality or any impurity or greed even be named among you, as is proper among saints; there must be no filthiness and silly talk, or coarse jesting, which are not fitting, but rather giving of thanks. For this you know with certainty, that no immoral or impure person or covetous man, who is an idolater, has an inheritance in the kingdom of Christ and God. Let no one deceive you with empty words, for because of these things the wrath of God comes upon the sons of disobedience. Therefore do not be partakers with them . . .

We learn several critical facts in verses three through seven. First, there should not be the slightest hint of sexual immorality or any kind of uncleanness or lustful impulses (greed) in the Christian community. Second, this applies to language and humor as well (v. 4). Third, people who are devoted to these things will be excluded from the kingdom of Christ. Fourth, don't be deceived about this, for this very thing brings down the wrath of God. Anyone who says otherwise is a deceiver, speaking empty words.

Verse four speaks directly to entertainment issues, especially with regard to comedy. The MacArthur Study Bible comments:

> These 3 inappropriate sins of the tongue include any speech that is obscene and degrading or foolish and dirty, as well as suggestive and immoral wit. All such are destructive of holy living and godly testimony and should be confessed, forsaken, and replaced by open expressions of thankfulness to God.

This truth, once understood by Christians, has been lost in our media-saturated age. Richard Baxter, the great Puritan, reminds us that filthy talk "is but thy breaking the shell of modesty, that thou mayest eat the kernel of the vomiting nut."

Now if we take verse four seriously, we must ask ourselves: When was the last time I exposed myself—or worse, my children—to such things? Why did I do it? For amusement's sake? How can that be justified? If indeed these things are "not fitting" and I am not to be a partaker with those who do such things, why am I participating?

One possible answer is that we have deceived ourselves about the corrupt nature of crude, vulgar, and obscene jokes. Comedies that reach into the gutter may be funny, making us laugh. *So it must be all right,* we think. Such a view is plainly against Scripture.

Another answer might be, "It doesn't bother me." But is "Does it bother me?" the right question? Wouldn't it be better for the Christian to ask, "*Should* this bother me?" The issue is about what *ought* to be, not about what is. To rely on what "bothers" me is trusting my heart, the very thing the Bible warns I should not trust. If someone steals or watches pornography enough times, it may not "bother" that person anymore, but is that a true standard? People do become callous. The heart is deceitful. A cold heart is not a reliable standard by which to live.

The words in verse four—*filthiness, silly talk,* and *coarse jesting*—certainly do describe the bulk of Hollywood's product. Even many so-called family films are full of these forbidden things. Do such amusements really violate Scripture? Let's continue on in the text of Ephesians 5, looking now at verses 8–12:

> For you were formerly darkness, but now you are light in the Lord; walk as children of light (for the fruit of the light consists in all goodness and righteousness and truth), trying to learn what is pleasing to the Lord. And do not participate in the unfruitful deeds of darkness, but instead even expose them; for it is disgraceful even to speak of the things which are done by them in secret.

You may wish to read verses eleven and twelve again before you proceed. It is logical to me—and I think the apostle would agree—that if it is disgraceful even to speak of these sexual sins—fornication, adulteries, perversions, etc.—then it must be downright shameful to *act them out*. If it is a disgrace to tell such things publicly, then to ask some poor actress to act it out for you is a manifest evil. There must be no compromise on this.

Is the Standard Objective or Subjective?

Questions that frequently come up when discussing entertainment standards are "Where do you draw the line?" and "How can you impose your standard for decency on others?" These are excellent questions. Naturally, I can't impose my standards on anyone. I don't have the power to do so. As far as where the line must be drawn, that is another matter.

There are such things as gray areas in the Christian life. Romans 14 discusses such nonessentials and the attitude we are to take toward them. Is morality in entertainment a gray area? Is it completely subjective? Is it one thing for me, and another for you? Are the Bible's standards like the world's— relative? No. Gray areas, as they are called, are areas where the Scripture allows us liberty. The end of liberty is sin, lawlessness, deeds of the flesh, and worldliness (Gal. 5:13ff).

If the Bible had nothing to say on the matter of worldly amusements, modesty, lust, coarse jesting, etc., the issue may all be reduced to personalized, relative standards. But this is not the case. The Bible is quite clear on these things. This is not to say there is no gray. Obviously, some things may be considered immodest by some (leotards, for example) while others see no modesty issue. These will have to be personal matters. But modesty certainly forbids public nudity, and this is supported by Scripture. It is not gray. It is not a personal standard.

What does the Scripture say? Let me invite you to take a serious look at the Bible with me. My only concern is that we let the Bible inform our standards and choices in everything. If you can read the Scripture and honestly pursue entertainments that I would suggest are morally evil, then you are free to pursue your will. It becomes a matter between you and God.

The Evil Message

The Bible is clear on the subject of evil messages:

> Woe to those who call evil good, and good evil; who substitute darkness for light and light for darkness . . . (Isa. 5:20)

Any amusement must be regarded as evil that mocks or attacks virtue, glorifies sin, or puts a positive spin on transgressing the law of God. A *woe* is the pronouncement of a curse. How, then, can God's people support with their money and time anything upon which God has pronounced a curse?

The 1998 movie *Pleasantville*, for example, using a clever mixing of black-and-white with color elements, boldly teaches that virtue is dull and that complete sexual freedom is what living is all about. Dishonestly mocking 1950s television, *Pleasantville* makes every effort to condemn the good and celebrate evil. The film's writers make the enormous leap in reasoning that since we didn't see people having sex on TV in the 1950s, their characters didn't know it existed. They didn't know where their own children came from. They have no idea what sexual pleasure is. That's why they live in black-and-white. Only hip, degenerate '90s kids can bring the color of sexual delights to that bleak world of virtue. This film tells us how far we have fallen in basic decency. It's amazing that filmmakers today cannot conceive of people existing who enjoy the pleasures of marriage but who keep their sex lives private.

Were Christians outraged by *Pleasantville?* No. While Isaiah's reaction would, no doubt, have been one of sorrow, self-examination, and repentance, many Christians supported this movie with extensive patronage. God's children were fed a diet of cleverly packaged evil. Evil messages, cursed by our Lord, should not receive our encouragement. What about evil methods?

The Question of "Tasteful" Nudity

This is the point in our discussion where Christian cinema enthusiasts start to get nervous. When you start talking about the Bible, a kind of fear grips them, and they believe they are about to be denied their favorite pleasure. Nudity in films is so prevalent that to forbid viewing it would take away the Christian moviegoers' "freedom." Knowing that the Bible will certainly condemn open displays of sexuality, these Christians ask, "What about a little tasteful nudity?" Does that fall under biblical condemnation, or are we just being prudes?

Nudity is a common subject in the Bible. When one examines all the passages with regard to nudity, a clear understanding emerges. The Scripture seems to have anticipated
our questions about nudity with simple, uncomplicated principles. Before we go to the Scripture, I would invite you to
cast aside your cultural preconceptions. Forget about Puritans and Victorian prudery and twentieth-century frankness
and the emancipation of the body. Step away from labels and
popular notions, and let the Bible speak.

We must begin at the beginning: Genesis, chapter two.
God created man and placed him in a paradise to guard and
keep it. God determined that the man should not be alone,
that he needed a companion that corresponded to him.

> And the LORD God fashioned into a woman the rib which
> He had taken from man, and brought her to the man.
> And the man said: This is now bone of my bones, / And
> flesh of my flesh; / She shall be called woman / Because
> she was taken out of man. For this cause a man shall leave
> his father and his mother, and shall cleave to his wife;
> and they shall become one flesh. And the man and his
> wife were both naked and not ashamed. (Gen. 2:22–25)

Genesis 2:24–25 is *the* foundation text on marriage in the
Bible. It is the text to which Jesus always returned in his
teaching on marriage. It describes two key elements of the
marriage union consistent throughout the Bible: (1) they were
naked; and (2) they were *not ashamed.* Theologians call this
the age of innocence. These two people had no bent toward
sin. There was no duplicity or covetousness. There was true
harmony. Nobody tried to use anybody.

Then comes chapter three. Man fell. He was immediately separated from God. He was *ashamed.*

> And they heard the sound of the LORD God walking in the garden in the cool of the day, and the man and his wife hid themselves from the presence of the LORD God among the trees of the garden. Then the LORD God called to the man, and said to him, "Where are you?" And he said, "I heard the sound of Thee in the garden, and I was afraid because I was naked; so I hid myself." And He said, "Who told you that you were naked? Have you eaten from the tree of which I commanded you not to eat?"

Adam's transgression, as he realized his nakedness, made him want to hide from God. Adam and his wife covered themselves, and God found them in that sorry condition. What did God say? "Oh, Adam! The human body is a beautiful creation. Don't feel like that! Now, come, cast away those fig leaves, and be innocent again." No. He did not say that. He never says that. God cursed Adam and Eve for their sin, and then

> The LORD God made garments of skin for Adam and his wife, and clothed them.

God personally stopped and made clothes for them to cover their shame. And from that point on, nakedness is always spoken of in the Bible as a shameful condition. There is only one exception: marriage, where the innocence of Eden is remembered, and the faithful intimacy of God with His covenant people is pictured. Outside marriage, nakedness—from the moment of The Fall onward—has always been connected to shame. Why did God make them coverings? Is God a prude? Doesn't He realize that the human body is beautiful? What's His hang up?

God designed the human body. He invented sex. But He knows more truly than we ourselves what our fallen condition has done to us. God is teaching Adam and Eve that clothing is a covering of their shame. Public nudity is an effort to deny human guilt and suppress the shame God wants us to have. People can be shameless, but only as a result of refusal to acknowledge our need for redemption. Privacy is also required because we have become covetous users of people. We see, and we lust. Our purity is polluted by our eyes. We are not to gaze on what is shameful: that is, another person's nakedness. We can pretend we are unaffected, but the Bible plainly expects us to respect the bodily privacy of others.

The Book of Genesis tells us that Noah, after the flood, made a fool of himself by drinking too much wine and exposing himself inside his tent. Alcohol, you may know, has a way of robbing a person of his sense of shame. Ham, Noah's son, found the sight of his father in this exposed condition a source of amusement. The Bible simply says, "he told his two brothers." Ham apparently thought Shem and Japheth would get a kick out of it too. But these men were of a different quality of character. Genesis 9:23 tells us:

> But Shem and Japheth took a garment and laid it upon
> both their shoulders and walked backward and covered

the nakedness of their father, and their faces were turned away, so that they did not see their father's nakedness.

They turned away. They did what God did, *covered* his nakedness because he was in a shameful condition. Shouldn't we, as well, turn away from the crude, the rude, the impure, and the shameful? It seems clear that Shem and Japheth are presented to us here as a godly example. It is not that their father was source of sexual temptation for them. His nakedness was a shameful condition, which was not to be a source of entertainment. It was something that needed respectful covering.

Who Invented Pants?

There seems to be a concern for impure thoughts in Exodus 20. This chapter, which contains major legislation beginning the Mosaic covenant, includes the Ten Commandments and laws governing the building of an altar. The final verse in the chapter says simply, "And you shall not go up by steps to my altar, that your nakedness may not be exposed upon it." God addressed an issue most people would be far too shy to mention. Steps led to a situation where people further down could see up the garments of those higher up. In a moment of high worship, a glimpse of nakedness might produce shameful or impure thoughts. Later in the Old Testament, when steps were included (Lev. 9:22; Ezek. 43:17), God said the priests were to wear pants under their robes (Exod. 28:42; Ezek. 44:18). As a designer of fashion—here and after Adam and Eve fell—the Lord had one thing in mind: cover up. Why is God so fastidious about this? Maybe He knows something about which we have deceived ourselves.

The Covenant of Purity

Job was a godly man. Chapter 31 of the Book of Job describes, in great detail, the moral and ethical life Job lived. It is his own declaration of the care he took to be a good and just man. It is one of the moral high points in the Old Testament. He talks about integrity, faithfulness in marriage, justice to his slaves, charity, faithful worship, and the treatment of enemies. But first on his list is purity. The words echo across the millennia:

> I have made a covenant with my eyes; how then could I gaze at a virgin?

A covenant with his eyes. What text could be more relevant to forms of entertainment that are almost exclusively visual? The question must be asked: In the light of this, how dare any Christian man gaze upon the body of someone else's wife? Or on the body of any woman who is not his own wife? Who do we think we are that we can do this in defiance of our duty to love all women as sisters? These are standards from the word of God. They are for us. Job was committed to a pure heart, and he knew that his eyes were the gateway to his heart.

Proverbs 6 warns about the evil woman. Solomon advised the young man very specifically on avoiding sexual sin: "Do not desire her beauty in your heart," he said (Prov. 6:25). He was talking about the young man's thought life—the images in his mind. To keep from her physically, you must keep from her mentally. That same chapter uses a common metaphor for lust: fire. Solomon compared one who lusts with one who holds fire too close to his breast: "Can a man take fire in his bosom, and his clothes not get burned?" he asked (6:27). You cannot hold impure things close. You cannot grant them entrance to the heart. A covenant must be maintained with the eyes.

The New Testament has no different ideas about this. Indeed, the strongest reinforcement of Job's covenant comes through the words of the Lord Jesus Himself: "Everyone who looks on a woman to lust for her has committed adultery with her already in his heart" (Matt. 5:28). And if we should be so tempted, Jesus said to take drastic action: "And if your right eye makes you stumble, tear it out, and throw it from you . . ." (v. 29). Jesus emphasized not what you touch, but what you look at.

The natural corollary to this teaching that was aimed mostly at men, is Paul's teaching aimed primarily at women:

> Likewise, I want women to adorn themselves with proper clothing, modestly and discreetly, not with braided hair and gold or pearls or costly garments. (1 Tim. 2:9)

Two important words are here: *modestly* and *discreetly*. The word *modest* is interesting; it means "with shame." Dress with the shame-consciousness in mind that God granted to humankind in the garden and encouraged our "first parents" to maintain. To dress with discretion is to dress with men's eyes in mind. Godly women don't dress to inflame lust, but to discourage it. For a woman to expose herself in a provocative way outside her marriage is sin. It is shameful. The connection to modern entertainment should be obvious.

The Hard Truth

Some will argue that brief nude scenes that are nonsexual do not violate these principles. I disagree. Even brief exposure to nudity diminishes our God-given shame consciousness. And lust is more demanding, more easily inflamed, and more prevalent than we care to admit. Bathsheba was not doing a striptease for David. The circumstances that caught his eye were normal and natural, but still his heart was set on fire through his eyes.

The truth is that cinematic nudity is a major cause of lust throughout our culture. I once worked in a film laboratory in Hollywood. Our job was to recondition prints of movies used in theaters. For many years, during my education, I worked as a film inspector. It was my job to grade the quality of the prints, inspect damage, count missing frames, and repair splices. After a time I began to notice a pattern, confirmed by the other inspectors. In films with even the briefest nude scenes involving women, prints by the dozens would come in from theaters neatly spliced at each nude scene. All over the country, pictures are collected for auto-erotic purposes by people who work in theaters or for film exchange companies. They do not collect beautiful faces or even frames with women in short skirts or bathing suits. It is the topless or nude figure that drives men to such measures.

Some pornographic men's magazines specialize in publishing pictures enlarged from these tiny frames of film. This means that an actress posing with her breasts exposed for a shot that might last five seconds on the screen is being used as a source of arousal long after the film is gone. Believe it or not, someone has written a book, describing in detail, all the nude scenes in Hollywood movies. A book catalogue describes its features:

> A unique alphabetical guide to nude scenes by film actors and actresses, thousands of entries list their films, rate the nude scenes in each, give the time they last and describe the type and quality of nudity in each. For adults only.

Every actress or actor who has disrobed for the camera is now publicly listed and graded. The writer for this book knows he has an audience.

We cannot pretend that these Hollywood movies with even brief passages of nudity and sexual acts do not have a morally debilitating effect on people. Men with pornographic addictions will often admit to an early use of videotapes of Hollywood movies, using the freeze-frame device to pause at an image long enough to accomplish a lustful act. These are unpleasant facts. But it's time for some truth. Nudity in "legitimate" films has led many souls down a path of grief and destruction. God knows. He has told us His way. We should not be deceived.

What about the nude male? Is that OK? If visual lust is a man's problem, maybe that is not as serious. In fact, however, there is no a substantial difference. The story of Noah should make clear that shamefulness is in public nudity itself, not mere sexual interest. Even so, there is a sexual interest in male nudity. Some women do find these images a source of lust. A female interviewer on *Entertainment Tonight* was practically orgasmic as she gushed over Keanu Reeves naked behind in *The Devil's Advocate.* "Was that your b———?" she screamed. "Oh, my God! It was great!" Reeves looked plainly embarrassed. And, of course, there are not only women who are sensualists, there are men inclined to homosexuality. I can tell you with confidence, they have not all sold out to their sin. Some are struggling with temptation, and they don't need male images springing up in popular culture either.

If Not God's Standard, What Standard?

If we do not adopt a biblical standard for entertainment, then where do we draw the line? Isn't this the age-old question for dating teens? "How far can we go?" they ask. Do we not encourage them to refrain from "bundling"—the old practice of lying alone together in bed with their clothes on? Do we not tell them, unequivocally, not to stimulate each other to orgasm or to engage even in petting that leads in that direction? Why would a youth pastor say no, without exception, to the idea of unmarried teens showering together? Does it not violate decency and purity of heart? Can we prove from the Bible that these things are unacceptable, even if they don't involve intercourse? I think we can, and it will be on exactly the same grounds that actors and actresses should not be undressed for us or simulate sexual activity. It is immodest, indecent, and impure. Period. How can sexual activity outside of marriage be black-and-white, all-or-nothing in life but in entertainment suddenly be considered in shades of gray?

There are pastors reading this book who enjoy and support worldly amusements. They see undressed women routinely. Let us ask them, if our entertainment standard is not the biblical standard, what will it be? What will you teach your flock? If it is morally OK, for example, to see *Titanic*—with a nude woman and a somewhat muted but plainly evident sexual encounter between unmarried people—is it all right to see two nude bodies together as in *Braveheart*? If that is all right, can we see a man stroking a woman's breast? Kissing it? Placing his hand or his body between her legs? Gyrations? These are all common, R-rated elements. Will you, pastor, tell your flock that these are acceptable? If not, *why* not? If so, on what basis? What is the standard?

The casual acceptance of entertainment content that is opposed to biblical principles is damaging the church and the culture. The movies routinely teach and glorify sin. In film after film, television show after television show, Christian sexual ethics are mocked. These amusements teach that when two people are attracted to each other, they must go to bed—the one inviolate truth of Hollywood. Even superheroes, such as Superman and Batman, bow to this rule. Some Christians answer, "So what? That's the world. What do you expect?" If nothing else, the answer to "So what?" is "Because of these things the wrath of God comes upon the sons of disobedience." What I expect is that anyone who loves Jesus Christ will shun this evil.

I do not question the pleasure these amusements can afford. That is precisely why this issue is one of deception. We have invited the devil into our homes and our hearts because he is funny, witty, charming, and comes holding

Oscars in one hand and Emmys in the other. Paul's conclusion in Ephesians 5:7 is "Do not be partakers with them."

Deception's Scourge

Deception is answered with truth. It has been my desire to tell the truth unvarnished. Let us not pretend, but let's call it what it is. John Bunyan, the famous author of *Pilgrim's Progress*, wrote another allegorical tale called *The Holy War*. The story describes the siege of a town in the manner of the warfare of the day. The warfare is allegorical. The town is called Mansoul, which is just what it says, the soul of a man. The one attacking is Diabolus. (You can guess who he is.)

As the story goes, Diabolus sends three agents into town to undermine Mansoul's leaders. Of course, these agents must go disguised, so Diabolus changes their names. One named Covetous is renamed Prudent-Thrifty. Another, Anger, is renamed Goodzeal. The last, Lasciviousness, is renamed Harmless Mirth. Under his old guise, Lasciviousness is often a guest in our homes today.

How does one answer such deception? What can one do? Simply stop going along with the ruse. Call them by their true names. When Mansoul turns to Christ, these deceivers are caught and imprisoned by the jailer, Mr. Trueman. The Truth. Be brave enough to call sin by its real name. It is not harmless mirth; it is moral filth. "Do not be deceived," warned Paul.

In our obsession with entertainment, we have omitted the most important biblical principle of all: the law of love. "Love," Paul tells us, "does not rejoice in unrighteousness, but rejoices with the truth." This principle of love deserves a full treatment, which you will find in the next chapter.

The Law
of Love

There's a scene in the classic movie *Casablanca* in which Rick, café owner and "big fish in a small pond," is approached by Annina, a young Bulgarian woman. She looks about eighteen years old and wants to ask him a question. Her face is radiant with youthful beauty, conveying a sweet, innocent quality, yet troubled by a painful dilemma. She is attractively but modestly dressed. Her conversation with Rick is as follows:

> *Annina*: Could I speak to you for just a moment please?
> *Rick*: How did you get in here? You're under age.
> *Annina*: I came with Captain Renault.
> *Rick*: I should have known.
> *Annina*: My husband is with me too.

Rick: He is? Captain Renault's getting broad-minded. Sit down. Will you have a drink?

Annina: No, thank you.

Rick: Of course not. Do you mind if I do?

Annina: No. Monsieur Rick, what kind of man is Captain Renault?

Rick: Oh, he's just like any other man, only more so.

Annina: I mean, is he trustworthy? Is his word—

Rick: Now just a minute. Who told you to ask me that?

Annina: He did. Captain Renault did.

Rick: I thought so. Where's your husband?

Annina: At the roulette table, trying to win enough for our exit visas. Oh, of course he's losing.

Rick: How long have you been married?

Annina: Eight weeks. We come from Bulgaria. Oh, things are very bad there monsieur. The devil has the people by the throat. So Jan and I, we . . . we do not want our children to grow up in such a country.

Rick: Er . . . so you decided to go to America.

Annina: Yes, But we have not much money, and traveling is so expensive and difficult. It was much more than we thought to get here. And then Captain Renault sees us, and he is so kind.

Rick: Yes, I'll bet.

Annina: He tells us he can give us an exit visa. But . . . but we have no money.

Rick: Does he know that?

Annina: Oh, yes.

Rick: And you want to know—

Annina: Will he keep his word?

Rick: He always has.

Annina: Oh, monsieur. You are a man. If someone loved you very much, so that your happiness was the only thing she wanted in the world, and she did a bad thing to make certain of it, could you forgive her?

Rick: Nobody ever loved me that much.

Annina: And he never knew. And the girl kept this bad thing locked in her heart. That would be all right, wouldn't it?

Rick: You want my advice?

Annina: Oh, yes. Please.

Rick: Go back to Bulgaria.

Annina: Oh, but if you knew what it means for us to leave Europe, to get to America . . . Oh, but if Jan should find out. In many ways I am so much older than he is.

Rick: Yes, well, everybody in Casablanca has problems. Yours may work out. You'll excuse me?

Annina: Thank you, monsieur.

I quote this scene at length for three reasons. First of all, it is an excellent example of writing for the screen. Second, it is a powerful example of good taste—Old Hollywood at its best. A child watching Casablanca would not know what Annina was talking about. Captain Renault obviously wants Annina to give herself to him sexually in exchange for exit visas. But notice how sexual terms are avoided altogether. Everything is said that needs to be said, but it is done in a manner that is tasteful and protective of the innocent. No one's moral sensibilities are assaulted. Third, and this is the point of this chapter, the actress is treated with respect. All the female cast members in *Casablanca* are treated honorably. They are treated as persons, not just as actors.

The other scene that tells us of Captain Renault's womanizing has no women in it at all. An officer comes in and says, "Another visa problem has come up."

"Show her in," Renault says, straightening his tie in the mirror.

Imagine, if you will, *Casablanca 1998*. How would Captain Renault's desire for the ladies be portrayed? Some young actress would be asked to bare her breasts, sitting in bed with him while he answers the phone, or some such scene, as Spielberg felt compelled to do in *Schindler's List*. Or perhaps even more explicit scenes would be filmed.

I don't even know the name of the young actresses who played Annina in *Casablanca*, but I do know that I have a Christian duty toward her. I am obligated to love her with the love of Christ. Part of the Christian love a man shows to any woman is in protecting her from being degraded or used in an improper way. By this rule, every time a Christian pays to see a film or rents a video that violates the innocence of the performers, he has done wrong. We affirm with our money the film producer's decision to misuse actresses like that young woman in *Casablanca*. Thank God, she lived in a day when such a scene was unthinkable.

Christians literally pay Hollywood hundreds of millions of dollars each year. Each dollar is a vote saying, "Yes, we want to see that. You may sexualize or undress these women any way you wish. I will pay for it." And so movies like *Schindler's List* or *Titanic* or *Braveheart*, whatever their worth as entertainment, become a cause of evil. Human beings are wronged in the making of these pictures.

When I was going through film school, I knew actresses who struggled with this issue. Do I take my clothes off for my career? Most didn't want to, if they could avoid it. If they could be in a movie like *Casablanca*—a good part, an opportunity to display their talents in a major feature without exposing their bodies—they would jump at the chance! But such opportunities are extremely rare today, and it is our fault that they are. We have voted for those who would shame these women.

As I mentioned in chapter four, I went through a stage when I believed, as most Christians do today, that if a film is good enough, it doesn't matter if some nudity or sex is thrown in. I didn't like it, but I accepted it. I was wrong; it does matter. My approach was selfish. Though I didn't want to see scenes like that, I was willing to tolerate them for a good time. I was placing my amusement, something completely unimportant, over my obligation to love, something of the highest importance.

I Changed My Mind

Two things shook me out of my compromising lifestyle. The first was seeing an R-rated film called *Excalibur*, director John Boorman's version of the Arthurian tales. It had many redeeming features. The story exalted truth, humility, love, forgiveness, friendship, and justice as the highest goods. Sin brought ruin to a kingdom: a good message. However, in telling the tale, Boorman included several nude scenes and one explicit sexual encounter. These shouldn't have been included, I knew, but because it had so many good qualities and lots of action, I gave it my stamp of approval. I even recommended it to friends, with a caution. I later found out

that the young actress, whose small role included this explicit and degrading sex scene, was director Boorman's own
daughter. I was sickened by this knowledge. I realized that I
had participated in an evil. I owed John Boorman's daughter
more than my patronizing her shame. I owed her more respect than her father gave her. I promised that this was the
last film I would support that used any woman in a way inconsistent with the law of love.

The second thing to awaken me to the reality of my
compromise was a brief text in the Bible. First Timothy 5:2
says to treat "older women as mothers, younger women as
sisters, in all purity." As a Christian man, this is my duty of
love to women. Young women are to be treated as sisters, in
all purity. From this I have developed what I call the "sister
test" in evaluating entertainment. This simple test has me
ask myself, *Would I approve if my sister were asked to behave
or expose herself in any way that undermined her purity?* No! I
would not approve. And I am duty-bound, by the law of
love, to extend that same disapproval of such requests to all
young women.

There are those who claim that seeing shameful things
in films does not affect them. They claim that their liberty
in Christ gives them the freedom to enjoy these things. I
say that they have missed their highest Christian duty: the
love they owe to others. They have an obligation to preserve the purity of the performers, and it really doesn't matter if the performers care or not. As Christians, we have a
kingdom-duty to be salt and light so these performers will
know someone cares about them enough to refuse to watch
their degradation.

Hey, I'm Not the Only One!

My decision to set a biblical standard for myself in this area found support in ways that surprised me. I read a wonderful book by two Catholic writers called *Movies, Morals, and Art.* In the book, Jesuit Harold Gardiner described a conversation he had with Fred Zinnemann, one of Hollywood's greatest talents. Zinnemann was working on *A Nun's Story* with Audrey Hepburn. Gardiner was concerned about a scene in which Sister Luke's character was to be examined for tuberculosis by a doctor in the Congo. Gardiner said he cautioned Zinnemann that the sequence should not in any way resemble a striptease. "Mr. Zinnemann looked at me in surprise when I raised this caution," Gardiner wrote.

"Father," Zinnemann said, "even if this film did not deal with a nun character, I wouldn't think of any such suggestion. I would not have the camera pan around to get a front or quarter view, just so outlines of a bosom could be glimpsed. I don't believe in such cheap stunts."[1]

Indeed, Zinnemann, like other great directors of earlier years, gave the world many excellent films without such "cheap stunts." Men of enormous talent can be men of moral integrity. Zinnemann's words are a floodlight of truth, exposing the Hollywood lie that nudity is artistic or "necessary for the story."

I was pleased to find, in a used bookstore, an 1835 edition of William Wilberforce's 1797 book, *A Practical View of the Prevailing Religious System of Professed Christians, in the Higher and Middle Classes in this Country, Contrasted with Real Christianity.* Despite the long title, the book is priceless as an example of the Christian conscience of a great man. Wilberforce, a member of parliament in the late eighteenth century, was the man most responsible for ending the British slave trade. He has long been one of my heroes, for he fought great battles for good, with love and tenacity. The purpose of his book was evangelistic—to wake up England's nominal Christians and show them their need for Christ. Then he wanted them to live for Christ, which required examining their lives for moral failure and compromise.

Wilberforce addressed many issues, and he did not neglect the theater. The risqué plays of his day, he found reprehensible. But in his call for Christians to abstain from theatrical amusements, he looked beyond its bad effects on the viewer. His great heart was really with the performers, just as it had been with the African slaves. Let me urge you to labor carefully through the difficult writing style of two hundred years ago, and consider these thoughts:

> *The Stage.*—We must here again resort to a topic which was lately touched on, that of theatrical amusements; and recommend it to their advocates to consider them in connection with [their] duty . . .
>
> It is an undeniable fact, for the truth of which we may safely appeal to every age and nation, that the situation of the performers, particularly those of the female sex, is remarkably unfavorable to the maintenance and growth of the religious and moral principle, and of course highly dangerous to their eternal interests. Might it not then be fairly asked, how far, in all who confess the truth of this position, it is consistent with the sensibility of Christian benevolence, merely for the entertainment of an idle hour, to encourage the continuance of any of their fellow creatures in such a way of life, and to take a part in

tempting any others to enter into it? How far, considering that, by their own concession, they are employing whatever they spend in this way, in sustaining and advancing the cause of vice, and consequently in promoting misery, they are herein bestowing this share of their wealth in a manner agreeable to the intentions of their holy and benevolent Benefactor? How far also they are not in this instance the rather criminal, from there being so many sources of innocent pleasure open to their enjoyment? How far they are acting conformably to that golden principle, of doing to others as they would do to us? How far they harmonize with the spirit of the Apostle's affectionate declaration, that he would deny himself for his whole life the most innocuous indulgence, nay, what might seem almost an absolute necessary, rather than cause his weak fellow-Christian to offend? Or, lastly, how far are they influenced by the solemn language of our Savior Himself: "It must needs be that offences come, but woe to that man by whom the offence cometh; it were better for him that a millstone were hanged about his neck, and that he were cast into the depths of the sea." The present instance is perhaps another example of our taking greater concern in the temporal, than in the spiritual, interest of our fellow creatures. That man would be deemed, and justly deemed, of an inhuman temper, who in these days were to seek his amusement in the combats of gladiators and prize-fighters; yet Christians appear conscious of no inconsistency, in finding their pleasure in spectacles maintained at the risk, if not the ruin, of the eternal happiness of those who perform in them![2]

I believe that Wilberforce's point is unassailable. This is the Christian conscience taking the law of love seriously.

Some modern Christian writers mock concerns over morals in such things as movies and television. Franky Schaeffer attacks Christians who call evil those movies assaulting decency. Abortion clinics, Nazi gas chambers, and genocide are evil, he says. "With runaway children being coerced into prostitution in our cities," Schaeffer wrote, "surely the evangelical-fundamentalist Pharisees who find time to print trivial 'Biblical' ratings of movies, could direct their pious energies toward issues of greater moment."[3] This is an unkind and unfair accusation, especially since Schaeffer himself wastes his time making forgettable films. The shallowness of his opinion is revealed in the preceding quotation.

Wilberforce, by contrast, who knew evil in its most virulent forms and spent his life energies fighting it, also knew that evil in the theater—in amusements that harmed the soul of viewer and performer alike—had to be addressed. His refusal to trivialize theatrical evils came from sound theology. He understood that anything that hurts the soul is evil, be it the slave trade or an impure amusement. Schaeffer, on the other hand, is unable to identify the evil of his own industry, including the corruption of its performers. Great men fight for and apply the law of love wherever it is needed.

Do Performers Really Care?

If we apply the law of love to performers, and choose not to support work that shames them—people made in God's image—do they care? Don't these actresses undress willingly? Don't they, with full compliance, let men press their bodies against them, grope them, and simulate sexual acts with them? The answer is no—not as much as you might think.

It's true that some actresses don't care. Modern Hollywood naturally attracts people whose sexual habits are degenerate. Some actresses regard sex as a commodity. Some enjoy being a tease. However, many do care. Many would prefer to operate under the rules of respect demanded by Old Hollywood when it was under the censor's thumb. Indeed, many actresses, after they become prominent and have some say in the productions they are in, refuse to "do nude." Others, to avoid shame or because they are determined to keep their bodily imperfections and aging a secret, insist that body doubles be used. These doubles are aspiring starlets who sell their naked bodies for use without their faces being seen. They become the disrobed bodies of name actors and actresses who refuse to humiliate themselves.

Perhaps the voices of entertainers themselves will help us understand. Although nudity has been common in films for over thirty years now, it is still a topic of interest. Articles still refer to how it affects performers. A few samples might include a 1991 Marilyn Beck column in which Virginia Madsen was interviewed about her refusal to appear nude in a CBS made-for-television movie. Madsen said, "Even if the audience isn't going to see you totally nude, you still have to be nude on the set. It's a real hassle." Madsen had done nude work in movies made for Showtime and HBO movie channels, but she finally decided she wasn't going to do it anymore. The column tells us,

> Madsen related that she succumbed to the "required nudity" pressure at first because, "To get your way you have

to get real pushy, and then you're labeled the problem actress. There's always like four guys standing around saying, 'What's wrong with the human body?' Nothing's wrong with the human body, but I don't really want to take my clothes off anymore."[4]

Madsen goes on to describe the pressure tactics used by directors. The word *pressure* is important. Taking one step back, we can ask, "What gives the director power to apply this pressure?" It comes directly from the patronage of these films (or ratings on TV). To be successful in America, a film needs the patronage of many Christians. Sadly, the pressure-wielding directors described by Madsen are supported with a substantial amount of God's money, spent by God's people.

Gwyneth Paltrow is only in her midtwenties, but she has appeared in many top Hollywood releases in the past few years. She made a wonderful impression in the delightful 1996 version of Jane Austin's *Emma*. Since then, she repeatedly has been asked to expose her body on film, and she has complied. Perhaps because her character in *Emma* was so wholesome and modest and because her performance marked her as a serious actress, Paltrow is often asked by the media about her nude scenes. During a publicity interview for *Great Expectations*, she told CNN that doing the nude scenes for that film was "daunting," but that it helped having a friend play her cinematic lover. It made the experience easier, she said. However, we weren't told if it was easy for him.

In June 1998, on Oprah Winfrey's television show, Paltrow discussed another movie in which she was required to expose herself. The conversation turned to Paltrow's family and their reactions to these films. "And when your father sees it?" Winfrey asked.

"I don't think he should see it," Paltrow responded.

Winfrey asked why Paltrow turned down the even more explicit scenes required for the movie *Boogie Nights*. "My grandfather is alive and healthy," Paltrow said, "and I want to keep him that way."

"Granddads don't like to see their granddaughters on the screen butt-naked," Winfrey suggested.

"No, no," agreed Paltrow.

The interview is revealing about what is really going on in these movies. We begin to see the performers as real people. What they are doing is shameful, and we can actually hear that a grown woman is ashamed to have her father see her work in a major Hollywood feature. For herself, Paltrow told Winfrey, "It's not my favorite thing, you know, to be nude, generally, in a movie. I prefer to be clothed."

Ellen Barkin has appeared in what Hollywood calls "A" pictures. These are major studio releases with large budgets and name actors. Of having often appeared in the nude— and even in some "steamy" sex scenes—she says in an interview:

> On some level I feel touchy about nudity. If somebody comes up to me and said, "Gee, I saw *Siesta*, it was really great." That's the first thing I think of. Instead of what my normal reaction would be, "Thank you so much," and *Gee, I guess they thought I was good in that movie.* No, I'm thinking, *Great. This person has seen me without my clothes on, and that's what they're telling me.*

The fact is Barkin senses that she is not respected as a person because of these scenes. She feels dehumanized and treated as an object. And she is.

Angela Bassett is a big enough name that she was able to refuse to be nude for the immoral film *How Stella Got Her Groove Back*, though many other actors in the film had to appear nude. Basset said,

> I didn't want to take all my clothes off on a big ol' screen for all the world to see, especially after all the attention I got based on my physicality in *What's Love Got to Do with It*. And that was just dancing and arms showing. I could just imagine what would happen if I showed up in my birthday suit up there.[5]

She regards as a burden the attention her excellent form has received, because the desire of Hollywood is to exploit her body, and she knows it.

Television's *NYPD Blue* is notorious for pushing network television into the R-rated tastes of subscription cable chan-nels. It is known that if an actor is a regular on *NYPD Blue*, he or she has agreed to nudity and sex scenes. It comes with the show. Gail O'Grady is a series regular and has submitted to the required nudity. She even received an Emmy nomina-tion. I was surprised to read the following quote from her in a newspaper interview:

> I'm not a prude or anything, but I find nudity distracting in films and television, particularly if it has nothing to do with the story . . . Then there's the embarrassment of standing

on stage with nothing but a little grape leaf and a pair of panties. Even with a closed set, you're still dealing with the director, the cameraman, and a few crew members.[6]

Plainly, in some important way, she feels used. Embarrassed at being exposed, she is experiencing shame, which is God's gift to protect her, but which she suppresses. She has compromised herself to get a lead on a top television show. She is not asked if she would rather not. The director will not even try to find a way to protect her, because he has a mandate to titillate the audience.

Now, we must understand what this means. If we participate by viewing these works, we take sides with those who exploit women, such as Madsen, Paltrow, Barkin, O'Grady, and thousands of others. We owe these women more than this. We owe them an opportunity to do their craft without being violated in this way.

The matter becomes even more serious when we consider that there are Christians in the entertainment industry. Our sisters in Christ are burdened by the same pressures. In a 1995 edition of USA Weekend, for a Mother's Day feature, celebrities were asked, "What's the best advice your mom gave you?"

Christian supermodel Kim Alexis Dugway answered: "'Remember right from wrong.' I used it when I started to model. There were times that I would be the only person in the studio who did not think it was a good idea to take my clothes off."[7]

In a Christianity Today article, Christian actress Marlee Shelton (Nixon, The Sandlot, Hercules) explains how moral principle has kept her from getting work. Many roles in Hollywood productions involve nudity, and she will not take the parts that do. "That's an issue that comes up often for female actors," she says.[8]

Any Christian has to respect Marlee's stand. But why is it "an issue that comes up often"? Because Hollywood succeeds with it. Christians and non-Christians alike pay to see films in which performers are pressured to display themselves in embarrassing ways. I believe the most practical expression of the law of love for performers is to shun works that misuse them. The law of love says to free performers from pressure to do evil. If the millions of Christians who currently see movies with nudity and sex scenes would stop tomorrow, Hollywood would change. The change would not be complete, but it would be substantial.

As a Christian, you must think about what is going on when you watch these shameless entertainments. You pay your money and a young woman is undressed for you. Perhaps she is handled by a man she hardly knows. Vulgar references are made in her presence—and you have paid for it all. Don't you owe her more than that? Whose side are you on? Should we side with the slimy "artist" or with the struggling actress trying to hang on to a shred of dignity? Let the law of love decide.

Meditations on the V-Chip:

The Moral Dimensions of Sex and Violence in Entertainment

The increasing prevalence of indecent material in our society over the past thirty years has led to national debates over how to maximize freedom for so-called adult entertainment and yet protect children from the flood of filth. In the 1990s, two forces have increased the intensity of the debate. One is the ever-increasing vulgarity and sexual looseness of prime-time television. The other is the technological revolution, which has made indecent material available through videocassettes, cable, satellite, and the Internet. One very recent "solution" has been the idea of TV ratings, advocated by politicians on both ends of the spectrum. These ratings will be connected to a blocking technology that has come to be known as "the V-chip."

It is interesting that the blocking device has been labeled the V-chip. The V stands for "violence." Indeed, in the media, complaints about the nature of television usually attack the more explicit depictions of violence than anything else. Public-opinion polls, however, show that most Americans want the rating system for sexual content and bad language just as much, if not more, than they do for violence. Town meetings—broadcast on C-SPAN—dealing with content ratings clearly showed that audience concern was directed toward sex and language issues more than toward violence. So why isn't it called the S-chip or the L-chip?

Commentators and major film and television reviewers warn us now and then about the violence in entertainment with an almost-eerie uniformity. On panel shows that investigate the healthfulness of TV viewing, these critics often are asked whether or not television's sexual content is too explicit. The responses, notable for their cookie-cutter sameness, usually fall along these lines: "No, I don't think so. I mean, I'd like some good realistic sex for adult viewers. We probably need more of it. Sex on TV is so cautious that it's downright boring! I think we spend too much time on the sex issue when our focus really needs to be on televised violence. How come these moralists never complain about that?"

Intimidated by the rhetoric of these "experts," many believers in traditional morality have accepted this emphasis. Conservatives, and even many Christians, will soften their criticism of sexually explicit entertainment by mentioning violence first. Some emphasize violence almost exclusively. Others employ a term that combines both subject areas: *sexual violence*, referring to the increasing use of degrading sex and rape as a subject of prurient interest. By protesting sexual violence, the traditionalist feels he has struck a blow against sexual explicitness without appearing to be a prude. Sexualized violence *is* an enormous social problem, especially in its effect on formative minds, since it directly associates sexual impulses with violence, spawning a new generation of rapists and perhaps an occasional Ted Bundy-like killer. But Christians should not diminish the far more common moral problem caused by licentiousness. It seems that purity is not enough to stand up for these days. So we have the V-chip to tune out violence on television. Of course it will function as an S-chip as well, but the message is plainly given: it is not "cool" to publicly lament sex on television.

A Needed Evaluation

All of this talk about sex and violence leads to some necessary questions. Are sex and violence evil in a dramatic setting? Is violence more harmful than explicit sexuality in programming? Are the two of these equivalent moral problems—merely two sides of the same coin?

While secular opinion may go to the contrary, there are substantial differences between these two issues. Therefore, sex and violence must be considered on the merits or evils of each, independently. What follows is an attempt to compare the issues of dramatic portrayal of sex and violence, using both a biblical and a rational analysis.

Some Similarities

One way to better see the significant differences between sex and violence from a moral perspective is to briefly consider their similarities. Both sex and violence warrant scriptural approval or disapproval based on the context in which they occur. Both have a role in the social order: violence for the security of the state and to establish the rule of law; sex for the unifying intimacy of marriage and the procreative need in establishing a family. Similarly, both have enormous, well-known potential for abuse and evil. Beyond this, however, the differences begin to stand out immediately.

Important Differences: Public Versus Private Acts

In considering the differences between sex and violence, the nature of the acts themselves immediately present immense distinctions. The sexual act (and in the Bible, nudity is nearly synonymous with sex) is by design a private act. Both morally and socially, the sexual experience was intended by God to be enjoyed within the confines of the sacred relationship and institution of marriage. "And the man and his wife were both naked and were not ashamed," says the second chapter of Genesis, and "the two shall become one flesh." Likewise, the writer to the Hebrews instructed us that "the marriage bed is undefiled." That is, in the context of marriage, sex is pure.

Contrast that with how Moses described forbidden sexual practices in Leviticus 18. Uncovering the nakedness of someone other than one's spouse, a euphemism for illicit sex, is labeled "lewdness," "wickedness," and "that which defiles." It is an abomination. Paul, in 1 Corinthians 6:18, gave fornication a unique status as a sin, setting it apart as the only sin that violates "one's own body." Since many sins can harm one's body, what else can Paul mean but that sex presupposes a complete giving of oneself? Sex involves one's deepest self. It is self-exposure, a revelation of one's essential being. To involve oneself in the nakedness of another, without the commitment needed for true intimacy, makes a mockery of sexuality.

It follows that the central requirement of privacy for the sexual act forbids its direct presentation in drama. To see the act is to pervert the nature of the act. To witness intimacy of this kind is to destroy intimacy (see Prov. 5:15–20 on marital intimacy).

The act of violence, on the other hand, is a public concern. Even when occurring in private between two people, it is a social act. The *Lex Taliones*—the eye-for-an-eye law of retributive justice—is predicated on the fact that all criminal violence is a social act involving the broader society. Not so, the sexual union.

Once this public/private distinction is understood, we can move a step further. Sexual immorality is *never* commanded in Scripture. God never violates the sacred place sex has within the marriage relationship. Such immorality is prophesied (2 Sam. 12:11), but only as a shameful consequence of sin. God's word is most consistent on this point. He never approves of nor encourages sin.

By contrast, violent acts are occasionally directly commanded by the Lord. Dare we too-easily forget commands, such as 1 Samuel 15:2–3, in which an entire people were to be destroyed? When Saul failed to kill King Agag, the prophet Samuel took it upon himself to hack Agag to pieces "before the Lord" (v. 33). Not only were violent acts commanded, but sometimes a violent act done on human initiative is heartily commended. In Numbers 25, Phineas, Aaron's grandson, went after an Israelite who brought a Midianite woman into his tent; Phineas killed them both. In verse 11, the Lord credited this action with having removed a plague on the people, because Phineas, the Lord said, "was jealous with My jealousy." There are many such examples in Scripture.

To restate the point: sexuality is honored as a private act exclusively, while violence is a social act in both its negative and positive aspects. Sex outside the secret chamber of marriage is never condoned, but an act of public violence for the right motive is lauded by God Himself. The two subjects are not equal.

It is precisely at this point of "public versus private" that our two subjects diverge. Both sex and violence have good roles in society, and both have potential for destructive misuse and misapplication. But note well the difference. Sex gone wrong is sex gone public. Sex outside the marital bond—and this clearly includes nudity—is a violation of God's purpose for humanity. It is an aberration—an evil. Violence, on the other hand, is to be a public act when it is good. Violence in the name of justice is always a public act in the Mosaic legal system. Private violence is the aberration. Personal revenge is to be avoided; it is evil. An act of violence that is proper can always be conducted in public without shame.

The Role of the Eye: To See or Not to See?

Let us now examine the sex and violence question from the perspective of the visual arts. Here again, we see a significant difference in how these behaviors are treated in the Bible.

Is Sex a Spectator Sport?

The eye plays a major role in the sexual life of human beings, especially in men. Sexual images are directly tied to the sin of lust in Scripture. King David had a serious problem with women, but it was *watching* Bathsheba bathe that drove him to his great sin. An awareness of the "lust of the eyes" is what caused righteous Job to make his vow at the most practical level: "I have made a covenant with my eyes; how then could I gaze at a virgin?" (Job 31:1). And, of course, Jesus went directly to the heart of the issue: ". . . everyone who *looks* on a woman to lust for her has committed adultery" (Matt 5:28, emphasis mine).

It is no surprise that Scripture approaches the male propensity to lust visually with a corresponding admonition to the woman: be modest (1 Tim. 2:9; 1 Pet. 3:2–4; Isa. 3:16ff). There is a direct link between a woman's mode of dress and male sin. This places an important social obligation on women.

Sadly, immodesty is the order of the day for the professional actress. It has not always been so, but it is in our day. Is it such a leap to apply all of these texts to the world of entertainment? No. The world is quite open about the purpose of immodesty in entertainment. It is to stimulate lust. Observe how many advertisements for films in the newspaper use the word *sexy* to draw an audience.

The Value of Viewing Violence

Violence differs from sex in that visually representing the violent act is not inherently sinful. As we have seen, there

are instances in which God calls upon people to observe violence, something that is never true of sex. When the Lord
smote the Egyptian army in the Red Sea, it was an event
God's people were to watch. Moses cried out, "Do not fear!
Stand by and see the salvation of the Lord which He will
accomplish for you today!" Likewise, when the need arises to
execute someone for high-handed rebellion against God, it
is to be a public act (Deut. 13:6f). Indeed, in verse 8, the law
says, "You shall not yield to him nor listen to him; and your
eye shall not pity him." In this act, "all Israel will hear and be
afraid." Far from being inherently sinful, the violent act is,
under certain conditions, recommended viewing.

It is clear, then, that while the expression of sexuality
and coital intimacy is never given an approved public context, the appropriate violent act has an appropriate public
context. There are three primary areas which seem to permit
viewing violence, and, by extension, dramatic representations of violence. Two have been mentioned: God's judgment and the human execution of justice, according to divine principles. The third area is the military.

It is an inescapable conclusion of serious Bible study that
the Word of God honors military prowess. The author of 1
Chronicles lists an "honor roll" of David's mighty men. These
are commended for nothing other than a soldier's loyalty and
feats of martial valor (1 Chron. 11:10f). Even the Philistines
are momentarily credited with heroic valor in capturing the
Ark of the Covenant (1 Sam. 4:7–10). The New Testament
gives specific mention of military ventures as acts of faith as
well (Heb. 11:33–34). Paul, too, in his well-known passage

on civil government, views the sword as something ordained of God to punish criminal behavior and establish justice (Rom. 13:1–6). It seems reasonable that these admirable deeds, honored in the full light of day, can be reenacted with benefit to the viewer.

The Vice of Viewing Violence

That some acts of violence are inherently appropriate public viewing is proven by the biblical approval of divine judgment, the execution of civil authority, and military endeavors. While this may be true, it must never be seen as giving blanket acceptance of violence as a means of entertainment. Violence in life, as in drama, can be the corrupt fruit of sheer exploitation, serving the least-noble passions in a person's nature. Many people have an inhuman, perverse attachment to violence for its own sake; that is, violent acts utterly removed from the noble qualities of enforcing justice, fighting evil, and demonstrating courage.

It may help the reader for a moment to place himself in the world of the early Christians. The Roman Christian had a form of entertainment unique to his age: the arena. It offered an unhealthy kind of diversion, universally condemned by the church. But true combat as entertainment was not as unreasonable as it sounds. War captives and criminals were destined for permanent captivity or death. The games were held whether Christians attended or not—and oh, the excitement! Why not attend?

Such was the temptation of Augustine's friend Alypius who, when literally dragged to the arena by his companions, at first refused to look upon the action. Augustine recorded the incident in his confessions:

> Upon the fall of one in the fight, a mighty cry from the whole audience stirring him strongly, he, overcome by curiosity, and prepared as it were to despise and rise superior to it, no matter what it were, opened his eyes and was struck with a deeper wound in his soul than the other, whom he desired to see, was in his body; and he fell more miserably than he on whose fall that mighty clamor was raised, which entered through his ears and unlocked his eyes, to make way for the striking and beating down of his soul . . . For, directly he saw that blood, he therewith imbibed a sort of savageness; nor did he turn away, but fixed his eye, drinking in madness unconsciously, and was delighted with the guilty contest, and drunken with the bloody pastime. Nor was he now the same he came in, but was one of the throng he came unto, and a true companion of those who brought him thither."[1]

Alypius was hooked, and many years of struggle lay ahead before he conquered his violence vice.

Is it fair to compare Alypius's tormented love of the gladiator combats with modern movies? There is a relationship. Violence for its own sake—the sheer sickness of the slaughter film, for example—seems to enliven the same passions associated with the Roman spectacle. There is no tale to tell, no enlightenment, no humanity, no virtues to encourage. It is blood, gore, and death for the sake of experiencing artificial terror or simply the pleasure of watching someone else's extremely violent death throes.

Of course, all of this can be quite entertaining, as was the arena, but does entertainment-value equal moral-worth? For many, this blood-drenched entertainment (such as the schlock horror of *Friday the 13th*, *Nightmare on Elm Street*, and their imitators) is humorous. For others, the exploitation-picture acts as a test of one's deepest fears: *Can I handle the fear and terror of this experience?* Unfortunately, passing the test leaves one with more questions than answers, for watching the film achieves a false courage that has no basis in personal values and poses no real threat.

Just as worrisome as the exploitative "slasher" movies, are the films that purport to be aiming at a higher purpose. Some of Hollywood's most respected talents have made names for themselves through an explosion of gore. Arthur Penn's *Bonnie and Clyde* and Sam Peckinpah's controversial film *The Wild Bunch*—both from the late sixties—radically changed Hollywood's presentation of violence. Peckinpah, in a news conference about his own movie said:

> My idea was that it would have a cathartic effect. No, I don't like violence. In fact, when I look at the film myself, I find it unbearable. I don't think I'll be able to see it again for five years.[2]

Martin Scorcese's *Taxi Driver* took cinematic gore to new heights. The film became part of history because of the fascination Reagan-assassin John Hinckly Jr. had with it and its costar, Jodie Foster. Reviewers and social observers noticed that, far from having a cathartic effect, audiences enjoyed the violent outbursts of *Taxi Driver*'s psychopathic character. Scorcese claimed he was shocked by this:

> Previously, I'd been surprised by audience reaction to *The Wild Bunch*, which I first saw in a Warner Brothers screening room with a friend and loved it. But a week later I took some friends to see it in a theater, and it was as if the violence became an extension of the audience and vice versa.
>
> I saw *Taxi driver* once in a theater, on the opening night, I think, and everyone was yelling and screaming at the shoot out. When I made it, I didn't intend to have the audience react with that feeling. . . . The idea was to create a violent catharsis so they'd find themselves saying, "Yes, kill"; and then afterwards realize, "My God—no," like some strange California therapy session. That was the instinct I went with, but it's scary to think what happens with the audience.[3]

Scorcese's fear subsided quickly. After witnessing the audience response to *The Wild Bunch*, he took the violence further himself. Then, after he saw a similar response to *Taxi Driver*, he pressed on. Scorcese has made a career out of extremely violent movies, notably *Goodfellas*, *Casino*, and his remake of *Cape Fear*.

Oliver Stone said that his extremely violent film *Natural Born Killers* (1994) is supposed to be cathartic as well. The audience is supposed to be upset with itself for enjoying the violence of this film, which some critics believe can't be topped in terms of pure gore. Stone says:

> It kind of sickens you; you pass through something, you burn off something, you cleanse yourself. There is no need

after you see this movie to watch more violence on TV. I mean, it's sort of like saying, When is enough, enough? You can walk away . . .[4]

This, of course, has not occurred. Hollywood continues to magnify serial killers, murderous couples, and sheer horror. There is no cleansing. The thirst is not quenched, just as it never was in Rome. Indeed, the arena produced a desire for ever more explicit and bizarre violence. The same is true in the modern arena of film.

Much of this explosion of violence is due to the anthropological beliefs of the filmmakers. Stanley Kubrick, whose *Clockwork Orange* was a truly perverse film inspiring copycat crimes in England, believes that "man isn't a noble savage. He is irrational, brutal, weak, unable to be objective about anything . . ."[5] Oliver Stone's advice on curbing violence is to face it. He believes children should be shown scenes, such as the apes pounding each other in *2001: A Space Odyssey*, and then be told, "This is what we are; we're animals. We were animals, this is our Darwinian chain; we have aggression in us."[6] Sam Peckinpah stated, "Churches, laws, everybody, seems to think that man is a noble savage. But he's only an animal, a man-eating, talking animal."[7]

This view of man as beast likely explains why these films have not been cathartic. They do not affirm, but deny our humanity. Like pornography, extreme violence desensitizes, making violence familiar and, after a time, no longer shocking. Afterward comes the challenge of finding the same perverse thrill.

Old Hollywood did not fail to express the terror of criminal violence. But it did so with limits. A scene from an early James Cagney film showed Cagney's character ready to murder a man seated at a piano. The man knows something is about to happen. We feel every bit of his terror. The camera pans away to Cagney's accomplice, and in his face we see the killing. Our experience is a human one, but we are not desensitized or attracted by the blood. Nor do we feel like cheering.

Much talk was generated by the extreme violence of Steven Spielberg's 1998, World War II drama *Saving Private Ryan*. Spielberg, regarded as a mainstream director if ever there was one, has bought into the belief that explicit content equals truth. Each director seems to advance the arrogant notion that his film will be the definitive study on violence. They all forget that next year, someone will try to outdo them. Spielberg even went so far as to claim that *Saving Private Ryan* was the first WW II movie that was not a slap in the face to veterans of that war!

What could he mean? Dozens of excellent WW II films, many made by eyewitness veterans themselves, have come out of Hollywood. Spielberg, who missed his generation's war, simply means that his film is bloodier than the others. But is it the amount of stylized gore that honors our veterans in drama, or is it our recognition that these men should be honored because they sacrificed life and limb, comfort and family, their lives and futures, for us? It is not the amount of on-screen blood and fire, but the humanity of the characters that lets an audience—cozy and safe in a movie theater—appreciate the real veteran.

Indeed, it could be argued that *Saving Private Ryan* suffers from fantastic and meaningless plot twists-and-turns, overwritten conflict between the men on the squad, and a fuzzy moral focus, as Spielberg seems to bend over backward to display Americans murdering prisoners. Would men on an urgent mission really take the time to watch a single German prisoner dig his own grave? Typical of modern films, *Saving Private Ryan* deals in extremes: extreme blood, extreme plot twists, extreme language, and extreme characters. One tiny squad includes the wisest and most sensitive captain (a captain in charge of a squad?), the coolest and most capable sniper in the world, and the worst coward in the US Army. These few men have more fantastic experiences in a few days than John Wayne had in a dozen films combined.

Compare *Saving Private Ryan* with a movie such as 1949's *Battleground*, and one can see immediately that Spielberg's raw-meat style doesn't win over substance. In *Battleground*, much of the soldier's suffering is simple deprivation—hunger, cold, and illness. Courage and cowardice are mingled in the same individuals, as in life. The battles are hazy. We are surprised by who turns out to be heroic and who is tempted to run away. The soldiers squabble, but not with over-dramatic speeches or with men quitting the war or by sticking guns in each other's faces—all cliches from lesser films, which resurface in *Saving Private Ryan*. Both *Saving Private Ryan* and *Battleground* feature a knife fight between a German and an American soldier. Spielberg's is extreme, showing the struggling men rolling over another wounded man with blood gushing in torrents from his neck. Finally we see the knife slowly entering the chest. In *Battleground*, we see only the men's feet as they struggle. It is creative, nonexplicit, and surprisingly powerful—surprisingly human. Does the explicit gore of *Saving Private Ryan* make us value the soldier more than the earlier, more tasteful film? I don't believe so.

Watching extreme violence does not add to our humanity, our virtue, or our appreciation of those who suffered it. Film is not real. It is art. As director and war-veteran Sam Fuller pointed out, the only way to really experience combat in a movie theater is to have someone behind the screen shooting real bullets at you. Then you can feel what they felt. Good taste does not diminish the truth of a tragic and bloody experience if the characters are real and their sorrow and loss are painted with brushstrokes of humanity. Increasing levels of gore only get tiresome and require ever more bizarre representations.

Even in real war, most soldiers become desensitized to gore rather quickly as a self-preservation response—to save sanity and brain power for the more important job of survival. Normal humans are not capable of unlimited, sustained concentration on horror. We have a built-in shutdown. How much more oversatiating is the violence of a movie that gives us the horror without benefit of the bracing survival instinct to force our thoughts away from the gore.

A Look at Limits

Between the approved contexts for violence in drama and the many clearly exploitative films, there are a number of movies that require personal discernment as to the appropriateness of viewing. Obviously, not all films of the horror genre can be classified as exploitation. Traditionally, the horror movie was not so much blood-soaked as frighteningly atmospheric. Monster films, such as 1931's *Frankenstein* or the science-fiction thriller *Forbidden Planet,* can even teach some thoughtful lessons about man. Similarly, the gangster film often presents a violent underworld life devoid of moral values. This is not to say that such themes must be categorically off limits. The question arises: Is it acceptable to portray acts of criminal violence that are of purely evil intent?

I believe there are certain settings in which violence can be shown without being detrimental to good morals. Since, by their nature, crimes are of interest to society, a reasonable exploration of the criminal mind or of man's darker side should not be neglected. A strong caution must be issued with this statement, however, and certain restraint should be observed by both the filmmaker and the viewer. Too often, a study of human evil becomes a fascination with evil itself. Some who dwell too long in Satan's domain forget the good that does exist in the world through God's grace.

All too frequently, the modern filmmaker crosses the line from enlightenment to exploitation—a line that can be leaped over rather quickly. The complete discarding of all studio codes of morality has allowed directors to lose a balanced sense of responsibility or concern for the ramifications of their work. It is interesting to note that several prominent directors from Hollywood's "Golden Era" did not regard the censorship codes to be restrictive, but rather saw them as an impetus to do better work.

The strange and biblically unjustifiable belief that "art needs no justification" has become a license for violent and sexual excesses. The Christian response to this must be one of caution and personal restraint. He must be more concerned for the state of his own soul and of society than for his personal viewing pleasure. This was the choice Alypius faced, and it became the decisive spiritual battle of his life.

While it may be difficult to draw absolute standards on the question of violence in art (much more difficult than the sexual areas), it would be foolish not to challenge ourselves on whether we are craving the savagery of the arena or building something better into our souls. It is certainly worth the effort to reject a morbid enjoyment of brutality for a choice of entertainment that genuinely reflects the human condition within a moral framework. There is a big difference between the content, tone, and intent of the violence in a movie like *Silence of the Lambs* and that of a movie like *Shane*. If we can't see that difference, we are in deep trouble.

What seems to be lacking today is even the barest recognition that there are limits in what ought to be done in these controversial areas. The need to press a little bit further for the same cheap thrill is a slippery downward slope. Man must strive for high standards, for his nature constantly pulls him toward baser things. There was a point some years ago when pornographers began depicting incest as acceptable sex. It was something they had said they would never encourage or even consider. But the desire for something new—the problem in the Roman arena, as well—pushes people into ever more perverse amusements.

Mainstream Hollywood faces the same problem as the pornographer—boredom. Talented but disturbed directors feel compelled to explore the most vile, perverse, and heinous things in which people can get involved. Man's corrupt nature, encouraged by limitless artistic freedom, makes this inevitable. Christians must not follow blindly along.

This does not mean, however, that there is a need for very many limitations on dramatic themes. Most of the problem really depends on *how* certain themes are handled. For many years, Hollywood confronted various controversial matters without graphic representations of sex or savagery, and the moral point was usually better made. Nothing has been added by being explicit, except the creation of jaded and needy viewers, always craving more. Plainly, some things are better dealt with "off camera," especially if the goal is not merely to titillate the audience or demean the actors, but to honestly examine how some experience or practice has impacted the character's life. This used to be handled through excellent writing, superior acting, and a masterful director's touch.

Still, the issue of *how* to portray sensitive themes is not the only consideration. Some themes are not suitable for artistic examination. The Scripture is so direct on this point as to be nearly overlooked. (Why does this happen so often?) A primer for any Christian involving himself in the artistic/entertainment world should be Ephesians 5:1–14, as I mentioned in chapter six. Of special importance is verse twelve, in which Paul told believers, concerning the unfruitful deeds of darkness, ". . . it is disgraceful even to speak of the things which are done by them in secret." If this is the case, it is more disgraceful to *act out* these "secret" things, and even more so to proffer them as entertainment! Clearly, some things are better left alone altogether. At the very least, extreme caution must be taken regarding any allusions to such evils. This passage, taken seriously, would instantly eliminate a whole class of the more recent Hollywood offerings, including many of those made by the finest talents in the business and seen by thousands of professing Christians.

Artists and entertainers are not free from God-ordained principles for the moral life. The artist's and public's desire to feed on themes of perversion and vileness is a clear sign of a culture in decline.

It's Only Acting

Another difference between sex and violence in the visual media has to do with the false belief: "None of this is real; it's only acting!"

Yes, it's true: it *is* acting. But actors are real people. A naked woman is just that. "Acting" like a naked woman may be done fully clothed. This used to be creatively filmed from the shoulders up, as for example, in *Gone with the Wind*, when Melanie is forced to give up her nightshirt to clean up a pool of blood. The shame of nakedness is portrayed by acting. Another example is *The Hiding Place*, in which the Nazi concentration-camp regimen requires the ladies to line up shamefully undressed. That shame is tastefully conveyed without exposing private areas. Similarly, an actor and actress doing everything short of intercourse itself to portray the sexual act are still two people naked (or nearly so), engaged in what, under any circumstances outside the marriage bed, is an immoral act. Critics might call such scenes "sizzling" and "steamy," but the New Testament calls them "deeds of the flesh," practiced by those who "shall not inherit the Kingdom of God" (Gal. 5:19–21).

Violence does differ from sex in this respect. A man shot on the screen is *not* a man really shot. That is acting.

Whether he receives a blow via a punch, a stab, a machine gun, or an atom bomb, it is still all pretend and special effects. This is not to say that all violent acts are acceptable on the screen, but it does mean that the term "acting" applies to sex differently than it does to violence. Casting notices in Hollywood trade-papers still warn potential performers whenever nudity is "required." Such notices are common, but few, if any, ever read: "Being shot, a must." One situation obviously involves the actor himself or herself in a way the other never could. Actress Angela Bassett, in discussing attempts by producers to induce her to perform nude said, "I remember Paul Reiser once saying [that] when you take your clothes off, you're no longer acting. It's a documentary."[8]

A Last Word

I would ask the Christian reader to reflect carefully on this whole discussion. I have tried to present here a point of view that is faithful to the twin swords of Scripture and reason. There are matters about which Christians plainly disagree, but at the same time, that does not preclude a call to holiness. The sad truth is that many Christians today have lower moral standards than did many non-Christians just a generation ago. That fact deserves careful consideration. Let's stop and think about what is right and where we are headed. The inspired instructions of Paul (from which the arts are not exempt) should be our guiding light:

> Therefore, do not be partakers with them; for you were formerly darkness, but now you are light in the Lord; walk

as children of light (for the fruit of light consists in all goodness and righteousness and truth), trying to learn what is pleasing to the Lord.

Language

American soldiers are running across an open area as they assault a farmhouse in France during World War II. German machine-gun bullets tear at the earth and men fall. An American twists and collapses to the ground. "I'm hit!" he cries.

His friend moves closer to him. "Where is it?"

"My back! I'm bleedin' to death. I can feel it."

The friend reaches to where a reddish substance oozes from the down man's pack. "You clown. Get moving," he says.

The man protests, "You can't leave a man. I'm wounded. They shot my back clean off!" "All they did was spoil your lunch," says the other, pulling out a dripping can of beans.

The mistaken soldier looks at the bleeding can, stunned. "Well, I'll be a dirty name," he says.

This is a description of a scene from the movie *To Hell and Back*, an autobiographical film of the exploits of World War II's most decorated soldier, Audie Murphy. The film was made in 1955, and it was enormously popular. Most people alive in 1955 knew that soldiers sometimes let slip a few expletives in the tension of battle. Not in this movie. Hollywood, under the censorship code, used "substitute" language. *Lousy* and *stinkin'* were common epithets in old war films. "Well, I'll be a dirty name" did not cause people to laugh this film out of the theaters or scream about a lack of realism. It did not hurt the box office. Indeed, the generation that saw life's starkest realities in two recent, bloody wars, didn't complain. It was understood: what soldiers might say on a real battlefield was inappropriate for the amusement of a mixed audience, especially in a film that would likely attract children.

The modern situation is exactly the reverse. On film, everyone swears and curses: men, women, and children. A typical, modern war film is a constant stream of the worst obscenities. This is done, it is said, for realism. Of course, in real life, soldiers are as diverse as ordinary citizens. Some swear a lot. Some swear a little. Some don't swear at all, such as real-life D-Day hero Waverly Wray. But modern Hollywood isn't about life; it's about decadence. It can be argued that there is so much bad language in modern films of all kinds, that any dramatic emphasis an expletive is supposed to carry, simply falls flat. It is not present for dramatic purposes. There is a more sinister motive. Even the presence of children does not make bad language less likely; indeed, modern Hollywood intentionally adds vulgarity to movies children are likely to see.

The Root of the Language Problem

Michael Medved, one of the few politically and socially conservative mainstream film reviewers, has made mention of the strange fascination Hollywood has with bad language. He says he understands sex and violence. There is a market for exposed flesh and a market for bloody action. But who, he asks, goes to a movie to hear bad words? What audience-need does it meet? Surveys show that people are offended by the bad language, yet Hollywood persists. Why?

The answer to such a mystery can be only speculative, but a reasonable explanation is not hard to find. Jesus said that "out of the abundance of the heart, the mouth speaks" (Matt. 12:34). This is the answer. The writers, directors, and producers manifest unclean, perverse hearts through their work. What flows out of their creative impulses is vulgar and impure, because their hearts are rebellious, vulgar, and impure. It is the same reason Hollywood can no longer depict people with sexual morals. They who worship sex and glorify it, cannot conceive of a life lived within a moral framework.

Bad language is expressive of a bad heart. Evil men curse God, curse luck, curse their circumstances. Gifts of God are verbally trashed. Even sex becomes a source of outrage as sexual terms are used as an extreme form of verbal assault. This is why a salvation experience with Jesus Christ often manifests itself most suddenly in a change of language. New Christians are surprised by the immediate transformation of vocabulary. This is because they have new hearts. It just isn't in them to curse God or His gifts when they live under the blessing of Jesus Christ.

What the Ear Hears

Is it acceptable for Christians to patronize movies that have bad language, especially when such language is a film's "only problem"? This issue is a little more complex than visually offensive content and morally deviant story lines. We have specific prohibitions in Scripture on what we should *see*. Certainly, to teach evil is condemned. We are also told what sorts of things we may not *say*. We have less-specific information on what we should hear, but even here, the Bible is not silent. Add to this the problem of the diverse nature of offensive speech. Several kinds of speech have been regarded as socially unacceptable. Four general categories we will consider are blasphemous speech, perverse speech, erotic speech, and crude speech. Then we will look at the subject of humor.

Words matter. The Bible warns us that the tongue

> is a restless evil, and full of deadly poison. With it we bless our Lord and Father, and with it we curse men, who have been made in the likeness of God; from the same mouth come both blessing and cursing. My brethren, these things ought not to be this way. (James 3:8–10)

Plainly, cursing men is morally evil. And of course, the third commandment is quite explicit:

> You shall not take the name of the LORD your God in vain, for the LORD will not leave him unpunished who takes His name in vain. (Exod. 20:7)

The question is: Is there any way in which such cursing might be appropriate in entertainment?

Let's begin our discussion with a review of several key ideas. First, the arts have a dual obligation to speak truth about the human condition and yet not be a stumbling block to men's souls. As mentioned in chapter two, there are two ways an entertainment becomes a worldly amusement. Worldliness is a fit label for that which promotes evil as good, and also for that which commits an evil in the telling of a tale, even if the overriding moral is good. It is evil to teach the blessings of adultery, but it is also evil to violate modesty and put on a sensual display in order to show the destructive nature of adultery. The world doesn't mind a lesson in morality if at the same time it can revel in sensuality. The real lesson is often taken from the image, not the story.

The important questions for language issues are really the same as for the visually sensuous images. Are the ears a channel to the soul, as the eyes are? Can language be a means of assaulting innocence? Does saying bad things have a detrimental impact on the morals of actors who must say them? If we say yes to these questions, then language clearly does become an issue for Christians in selecting appropriate entertainment. Yet, since there are, it seems, different kinds of bad language, I believe we should examine each kind according to the questions above.

Blasphemous Speech

I would imagine that any believing Christian would be pained to hear the name of God or the Savior Jesus Christ being used as an expletive. People who are angry shout out words associated with excrement, sex acts, and the divine name. It is hard to imagine such language being worthy of the word *entertainment*. It is only in the last few years that television allowed God's name to be connected to the front of the word *damn*. The name of Jesus, too, is used in many films as a curse word. I don't believe such sin could be permitted as a means of entertainment. The third commandment holds the solemn warning: "The LORD will not hold him guiltless who takes His name in vain."

I do think that, as art should convey truth, a character might express anger at God or curse the heavens for some meaningful purpose of the story. But the throwaway use of God's name as profanity is simply unacceptable. All of us would be in the streets, organizing protests, if our mother's name were used that way. Why do we accept it of our most precious heavenly Father?

Perverse Speech

The use of sexual terms as profanity has traditionally been regarded as among the most offensive forms of speech, right up there with blasphemy. This is because sexual terms degrade God's gift and attack innocence at the same time. Such abuse of this special part of life has the effect of blending sex—a private and precious thing—with intense hostility and hatred. The intent is to shock and humiliate. Again, such speech has no place in what we call "entertainment."

Erotic Speech

This form of speech has turned into a multimillion-dollar industry as phone lines are used for purposes of sexual arousal. A film conceivably could depict no sexual acts or nudity, but be just as morally debilitating through suggestive or explicit sexual banter. The fact that this is big business in

the "sex industry" is proof enough of the sensual lusts connected with mere words.

Such speech outside the marriage chamber is categorically condemned in Scripture:

> For speaking out arrogant words of vanity they entice by
> fleshly desires, by sensuality, those who barely escape from
> the ones who live in error, promising them freedom while
> they themselves are slaves of corruption; for by what a
> man is overcome, by this he is enslaved. (2 Pet. 2:18–19)

Sensuality is a trap whether it is presented to the soul through
the eyes or the ears. Any entertainment that uses erotic speech
attacks innocence and generates impure thoughts and desires. It is sin.

Crude Speech

Some words have been considered inappropriate for polite company. If anyone describes a cad as a "son of a mule,"
not an eye is blinked. But substitute for *mule* a word for a
female dog, and that is using bad language. Kenneth Taylor
got in hot water for using such a term in his Living Bible
translation. It is easy to build a biblical argument for not using such language, because the Bible sets a clear standard:

> Let your speech always be with grace, seasoned, as it were,
> with salt, so that you may know how you should respond
> to each person. (Col. 4:6)

Certainly, any speech, on our part, should not violate the
rules of common decency. That would not be salt. It would
not be gracious. It would not edify (see Eph. 4:24).

Such speech in entertainment, I regard as a lesser offense than first three categories. But still, the use of such language in movies does tend to facilitate its acceptance in general society. Let's face it: what movie stars do, the impressionable imitate. It would be very welcome, indeed, if Hollywood returned to a time when soldiers called themselves "a dirty name."

Filthy Humor

One type of speech on which the Bible is very clear is crude or sex-based humor. Dirty jokes are forbidden. Ephesians 5:4 states,

> There must be no filthiness, or silly talk, or course jesting, which are not fitting, but rather giving of thanks.

The dirty joke, which dominates television humor and is common in nearly all films today, is unacceptable entertainment. Humor is a particularly sinister way of tearing down innocence. Laughter in itself is a kind of approval, and immoral humor is a clever way to get people to affirm and approve what they otherwise would not. It is hard to keep a moral guard over one's heart while laughing. Humor opens a door for impurity.

Because the Bible is so clear, proper diligence must be taken here. Most modern movies—even many PG films—contain humor that falls under the prohibition of Ephesians 5. A recent Disney movie, with television actor Tim Allen, had in its theatrical preview, jokes referring to the size of sexual organs. The film was aimed at families and was rated PG. Parents especially must exercise caution and hold firmly to a biblical standard.

In My House

As one who holds to the high-standards view with re-gard to entertainment, language questions pose endless di-lemmas for me. In our home, just as we will not view any film that has nudity or sexual acts depicted, we will not allow films with erotic, perverse, or blasphemous speech. We will not allow dirty jokes or vulgar humor. Naturally, most of our film choices are classics, made between 1935 and 1965.

We do, however, make certain allowances for speech that is regarded as impolite. We had to draw some kind of line, so I have an entirely personal measure I call the "*True Grit* stan-dard." In the John Wayne movie *True Grit*, "The Duke" plays a pretty salty character named Rooster Cogburn. This US marshal uses some rough language. There is no sexual banter or dirty jokes, but he does use a few *damns* and *hells*, and he calls one of the bad guys that alternative for "son of a mule." I would rather the film use no such words.

But *True Grit* is an excellent film with many redeeming fea-tures, most notably the character of Mattie Ross. It is extremely rare to have such a strong female lead and no romantic subplot. This teen heroine uses no bad language—unless you count the withering "You sorry piece of trash." She sharply rebukes Mar-shal Cogburn for drinking, and she makes several references to her Christian faith. The Marshal's faults are seen as faults. Had Mattie's character been equally vulgar, without providing a con-trasting goodness, we likely would have rejected this film.

So here I am, balancing a good and, at its heart, decent film, with concerns over some rough language. Curiously, *True Grit* was rated G, despite its rough language and some bloody violence. I think this (I believe inappropriate) rating can be explained by the overall wholesome nature of the film. But

the sort of language that occurs in *True Grit* is about as far as
I'll go. It is the maximum allowable for us. Again, this is a
personal decision, weighed carefully against an honest ap-
praisal of biblical ethics and artistic concerns. Every Christian needs to wrestle with these issues. Not everything is cut-
and-dried. I would not think anyone "legalistic" for erring
on the side of caution and disallowing *True Grit* for their
viewing. In this case, however, I choose to believe the film's
merits outweigh speech that is essentially impolite.

Now, lest I be accused of dumping the high-standards view
(discussed in chapter four) for the engagement view (i.e.,
anything's OK for art's sake), I must explain the difference. The
high-standards view is rigorous about issues to which the Bible
speaks clearly. I believe that with regard to speech, some matters are clear and others less clear. The use of *damn* by Henry
Higgins in *My Fair Lady*, for example, is simply not the same as
if he were using some explicit sexual terms, excretory terms, or
put God's name on the front of the thing he were damning. His
use of the word is not excessive; it serves a purpose and is offset
by the many other characters who never swear. The same could
be said for Clark Gable's famous last line in *Gone with the Wind.*
Impolite speech in drama, I believe, is not the same as filthy
humor, or blasphemous, erotic, or perverse speech.

Christians must never blatantly embrace what the world
offers. Entertainment from the world demands a careful ap-
praisal. That which is plainly evil must be rejected. That
which is questionable must be weighed carefully. And even
more careful consideration must be given to material that
will be viewed by children, who are impressionable and still
forming their beliefs and values. The next chapter discusses
the very important need to protect our children's innocence.

Stumbling Blocks

I couldn't sleep, assigned as I was by my host to an uncomfortable sofa. I was spending the night at a relative's house over a holiday, with several other families. It wasn't the sofa alone that kept me awake. I had to contend with the snickers and adolescent conversation of a small group of boys who were supposed to be finding their own repose on the floor. In the blackness, the young voices were animated, discussing a movie they all had seen. I don't know what the title was, whether or not it had any action, strong characters, or a moral to the story. These boys were between nine and eleven years old, and they had only one thing on their minds: how much of the "private" areas they had been able to see of some actress. The conversation revealed this as the only point of interest. All else was swept aside by an image upon a screen of an unattired woman.

No doubt the world would regard such a conversation as cute. Here are preadolescents exploring their interest in a budding sexuality. A less worldly point of view might see here the seeds of a sexuality awakened before the appropriate time. This view might be concerned with a sexual nature that might one day go out of control (and in fact, did), resulting in promiscuity, pregnancies, torn-apart relationships, and sorrow. As we have said, the Bible emphasizes over and over the role the eye plays as a means of inflaming lustful passions. Hollywood understands this, of course, as a business advantage. To make money, the talented people tease and please the passions that lay dormant, even in the young.

As a pastor, I've counseled many people who have problems controlling their sexual urges. A common pattern emerges in the history of these people. There was often, especially among men, an early exposure to visual material that excited their sexual instincts. It may have been ads for lingerie or undergarments in a catalog, erotic images in women's magazines, the *Sports Illustrated* swimsuit edition, television shows, movies, or a combination of these. Young minds seize on these images, use them to find a sexual release, and become permanently attached to such impulses. They have no idea that the road ahead may include an unsatisfactory sex life in marriage, or a future wife's broken heart as she discovers the secret. The amount of suggestive images in day-to-day popular culture explains why the hard-core porn business rose from a ten-million-dollar-a-year business in the 1960s to an eight-billion-dollar-a-year business today. Small fires become great conflagrations.

Traditionally, it has been understood by Christians that anything that inflames lust—inordinate desires—is evil. This is because Jesus' words were taken seriously:

> everyone who looks on a woman to lust for her has committed adultery with her already in his heart. (Matt. 5:28)

Obviously, things that inspire lust in the young are particularly offensive, since these things overthrow innocence and derail purity in those who are seldom mature enough to resist. The images need not be explicit. An immoral message, alone, is a stumbling block to the young. Imagine being a child of ten or eleven when 1980's *Superman II* hit the screens. A PG movie, its plot unfolded with the usual villains and special effects. For a while, Superman loses his powers. Soon after, we see him in bed with Lois Lane, both characters obviously undressed. What are they doing in bed together? They've had sex. What does a young mind do with this image, this knowledge? The movies have just given a definition of love in modern cultural terms, which simply means sex.

The child does not say, "Oh, too bad they put that in there. What a cheap stunt." No! This is Superman, a hero! There is conflict within the child. He is attracted to the hero. Superman is the *good* guy. He wants to root for him, yet here he is a fornicator. Some part of the young viewer, desperately wanting to defend his hero, whispers to his soul, *Well, it can't be such a bad thing.* That thought compromises his innocence.

One of the most cynical things I have ever read in my life was an interview with screenwriter Mario Puzo in a May 1979

issue of *American Film*. Here Puzo described the compelling
artistic reasons Superman had to bed Lois in the second film:

> . . . I think the second movie will be better than the first
> movie: it will have more of my stuff in it. It will be a better
> story anyway. In the next film he becomes mortal. I worked
> that out just so he could get into bed with Lois Lane. I
> figured you had to have that—well, I had to have that.

The direction of the story was taken down this path simply
to please a twisted man's desires. There's a perverse delight
in being the tempter of youth. Puzo's religious views come
out in the same interview. He said it was a silly idea to have
Superman be able to go back in time:

> You doubt if he can do it, no matter how strong he is. If
> he can do that, he can do anything. Why not turn it back
> two thousand years and save Christ and save us all a lot of
> trouble?

What is remarkable is that many Christian parents saw no
need to protect their innocent children from this movie. It is
still seen in Christian homes on television to this day.

Biblical language describes enticements to sin as "stumbling blocks." The picture is of a person walking along and
then being caused to fall by some well-placed obstacle. They
are tripped up. Jesus reserves a horrific picture of punish-
ment for those who place stumbling blocks before any of
His "little ones":

> Whoever causes one of these little ones who believe in
> Me to stumble, it is better for him that a heavy millstone

be hung around his neck, and that he be drowned in the
depth of the sea. Woe to the world because of its stumbling blocks. For it is inevitable that stumbling blocks
come; but woe to that man through whom the stumbling
block comes! (Matt. 18:6–7)

Stumbling blocks will come. They must come in a fallen
world. But a woe is pronounced upon those who bring such
obstacles. The curse of God is upon them. One imagines, at
the return of Christ, a long line of millstones stretching from
Hollywood to the Santa Monica pier. Creators of perverse
entertainment—impure, degraded language and lust-inspir-
ing images—must stand before the holy God and Father of
the children who have been made to stumble.

More frightening, and most tragic of all, is the complic-
ity of Christian parents in placing before their children's
eyes—and thus driving into their hearts—sexual images and
filthy humor, which tears down their God-given inhibitions
and shreds the fabric of their innocence. Living in our culture, our children will face these stumbling blocks. They will
see billboards and magazine covers in the supermarket that
target the flesh. It is likely they will be exposed, somewhere,
to children who have access to pornography. They may catch
a television show, a commercial, or see a video in an unsu-
pervised moment. Stumbling blocks come. But we live in an
age when parents, even Christian parents, purposely and
knowingly expose their own children to immorality. These
same parents are shocked later when they discover their children are sexually active. They can't understand how their
child could have been so unwise.

It is difficult to understand why biblical teaching and parental practice don't connect in this area. In conversations with Christians on this subject, I generally hear two broad rationalizations. First, some parents think there may be a problem, but it is not serious enough to change their habits. They believe that since this is the world we live in, everyone needs to deal with it as they can. This view is a lazy one and reflects how effectively the world has inched its way into the Christian heart. I believe that education on the issue of worldly amusements can awaken many of these Christians to repent of being a stumbling block to their children.

Second, some parents have persuaded themselves that children have no interest in or understanding of sexuality and, therefore, remain untouched by it. Lurid comic situations, women in provocative clothing, or characters speaking in obscene ways has no influence on children, they assume, because the children "don't get it." This common error defies common sense. One need only listen to children on the playground to realize how much they do understand. Recent studies have shown that children comprehend many of the lurid sexual innuendoes so frequent on network television. Even when they don't make a specific connection, children are very aware that "naughty" speech is the source of great fun among adults.

Many children in our culture have mental references for the innuendo because they have seen the real thing. The movies, HBO, movies of the week, and many television programs are so explicit that even young children possess a good deal of carnal knowledge. They are already sexualized beyond their years. Neil Postman, in his excellent book *The Disappearance of Childhood*, explains why this is so:

Television . . . is an open-admission technology to which
there are no physical, economic, cognitive, or imaginative restraints. The six-year-old and the sixty-year-old are
equally qualified to experience what television has to offer. Television, in this sense, is the consummate egalitarian medium of communication, surpassing oral language
itself. For in speaking, we may always whisper so that the
children will not hear. Or we may use words they may not
understand. But television cannot whisper, and its pictures are both concrete and self-explanatory. The children see everything it shows.[1]

This last sentence is exactly the point. To see is to know. It
may not be to know as an adult knows, but that is all the
more destructive. There is not the maturity to resist or to
know what to do with the shame of being exposed to private,
intimate matters.

Tragic Confirmation

Everything Postman said was powerfully confirmed to me
in May 1995. Two back-to-back experiences pushed me to
start teaching on the subject of entertainment in depth.

The first incident was catching an episode of ABC's *20/
20* program, aired May 10, 1995. The first segment was called
"Age of Innocence" and was introduced this way by Diane
Sawyer:

A producer on our show noticed that her daughter was
talking about wanting to be sexy . . . and her daughter was
only three. So we started asking around and discovered that
parents and a lot of teachers think something new has be-

gun among very young children—something that challenges the time-honored idea that all the sex on TV, in the
movies, and magazines is going right over their heads.

Now we all know that kids have a natural curiosity
about sex. They ask questions. But we're talking about
something different here—more about attitude—an attitude starting very young.

What follows is a brief documentary on the sexually satu-
rated minds of modern children. It is startling, eye-opening,
heartbreaking, and it explains so much.

The producer's three-year-old daughter was captured on
video choosing costumes for Halloween. She pointed to a
revealing, grown-up picture. "Why that one?" her mother
asked. "Because I like the sexy of it," the girl replied. This
exchange was followed by an interview with teachers about
changes they have seen in children over the past few years.
One read a second grader's love note, which concluded, "Let's
go to a hotel. I want a sex with you." The documentary then
turned to a brief review of animated heroines and how their
bodies have changed since *Cinderella* and *Sleeping Beauty*.

The most remarkable portion of the documentary took
place in a Syracuse University observation room. Here, typical kids were invited to be interviewed by researchers. The
children's parents watched from another room as cameras
secretly taped the research sessions. First, the children were
shown some scenes from two hugely successful Jim Carrey
movies: *The Mask* and *Ace Ventura: Pet Detective*. Both films
were rated PG-13, and most of the children—even five year
olds—had already seen them. *20/20*'s viewers were reminded

that these films contain "the lengthy bed scene, the oral sex scene, and the finale, where a woman turns out to be a man." Diane Sawyer narrated: "Is it true, we wondered, if the racy scenes in these movies go over our kids heads."

Six-year-old boys howled over scenes in *The Mask*. "It's the wild thing," one boy intoned. During the showing of a bed scene, little girls in a group (aged five to seven) said, "They're having S-E-X." "They are naked!" shouted another girl. But a seven year old explained it all: "I mean, they're actually having sex because in the bed, if they're lying together . . . they have to go on top of each other . . . and remember, they're naked, right?"

The researcher asked, "Does it bother you when you see that?"

"Yeah," she said, "because if little kids watch it, like my little brother, he thinks its OK."

Out of the mouths of babes.

Watching scenes of the ridiculously voluptuous Jessica Rabbit (from the Walt Disney feature *Who Framed Roger Rabbit?*), six-year-old girls were asked what effect she had on men. One tot piped up, "They like her and they want to marry her." Another six year old begged to differ: "Not if she sticks her boobs in their face." Still another girl said, "You gotta show them if you want to have a baby." And these were not the most upsetting moments.

A child-development expert was interviewed and stated that the sex-saturated media is "changing their self-perception. It's changing their self-esteem. It's changing what they talk about with each other."

Several children were shown in a playroom before they met with researchers. The room was full of toys and also had a few videos. The video tapes were mostly of cartoons and children's stories, but there was a Cindy Crawford exercise video, as well. The Crawford tape, with her gyrating to music, was by far the "toy" of choice. One nine-year-old boy cradled the video in his hands and chanted a song from a commercial, using his own lyrics: "Shake that body. Rip off that swimsuit. Rip off that swimsuit for me."

Cindy Crawford responded to this broadcast in a USA Today article, claiming she was "freaked out" by the sight of the boy with her video. She said, "It's tough. I'm in an industry which kind of gives them these images." Kind of.

The same boy was featured with several others in a research segment on magazine models. Children were shown images of models: one provocatively dressed, one more conservatively. Although the models were often the same person, the children thought the scantily clad models were prettier. The boy who earlier had held the Crawford video, stared at a magazine model who was wearing a revealing party dress. His nine-year-old mind struggled to bring together the morals he had been taught with what his media-excited libido craved. He liked the woman, he said: "She looks you in the eye. She's probably not snotty. Like one of the Ten Commandments: Thou shalt honor thy father and thy mother. She'll respect her parents, her husband, all those." His young mind could not sort out adult pleasures from moral virtues. He was already corrupted.

I was devastated by this documentary. I taped the segment and have been able to use it as a teaching tool on several occasions. But the questions still haunt me. If the influence on the minds of children is so pervasive, what hope is there? Why has the church been so silent on this issue? Christian homes have video shelves loaded with these movies—stumbling blocks laid right before the eyes of our own children. The *20/20* episode's expert, near the end, stated, "I see that they're starting to get hooked. They're getting hooked into these kinds of images, and they're going to need more of it."

An experience I had the day after the airing of the *20/20* segment, brought these startling facts to life. Home-schooled children are, so I believed, more protected than the average child; they are more innocent. My children are home-schooled. This particular day was library day. About thirty of us from our support group went to the public library. After we arrived and heard a story, the kids spread out to find books of interest. Some of the boys, between ages seven and nine, went straight to the magazine rack in the children's area. There were magazines for skateboarding, motocross, sports, nature, airplanes—all kinds of things to interest them. These boys, however, knew what they wanted. They pulled out a copy of *Sassy*, a magazine for teenage girls. They took it back to a table, and the nine year old found all the pictures of models with low-cut dresses, bare midriffs with several pant buttons undone, and anything else that smacked of sex. He was hooked. He pointed and he leered. He was passing on his interest to his seven-year-old brother and a friend. I was shocked. Where does such an interest begin at so early an age?

The Law of Diminishing Returns

Obsessions and addictions are dependent on getting people to partake once; then the pleasure of the experience

brings them back again. The boredom of the same exact experience after a few repetitions moves them to go farther and
deeper to get the same thrill. This is why youth ministers tell
young people to refrain from petting and stimulating their
boyfriends and girlfriends to states of arousal. The pleasure
induces a desire for more. Biologically, the body is designed
so that sexual stimulation will lead to intercourse. Getting
started and trying to stop defies biology and becomes a
herculean task. It is better, of course, not to begin at all.

We have discussed the fact that human males are particularly susceptible to states of arousal from what they see.
Consider the following statistics from the February 1997 issue of US News & World Report:

> Twenty-five years ago, a federal study of pornography
> estimated that the total retail value of pornography in
> the United States was no more than $10 million, and per-
> haps less than $5 million. . . .
>
> Last year Americans spent more than $8 billion on
> hardcore videos, peep shows, live sex acts, adult cable
> programming, sexual devices, computer porn, and sex
> magazines—an amount much larger than Hollywood's
> domestic box office receipts and larger than all the rev-
> enues generated by rock and country music recordings.
> Americans now spend more money at strip clubs than at
> Broadway, off-Broadway, regional, and non-profit the-
> aters; at the opera, the ballet, and jazz and classical mu-
> sic performances—combined.
>
> The number of hard-core video rentals rose from 75
> million in 1985 to 490 million in 1992. An all time high
> was reached in 1996 with 665 million rentals made in
> one year . . . Every night, between the peak hours of 9:00

P.M. and 1:00 A.M., a quarter of a million Americans pick up the phone and dial a number for commercial phone sex. In 1996, Americans spent between $750 million and $1 billion on phone sex. . . .

[On the Internet] *Playboy's* web site, which offers free glimpses of its Playmates, now averages about 5 million hits a day.[2]

These statistics reflect the dimensions of only the legal sex industry. Of course, many have moved beyond the legal to frequent prostitutes and other unmentionable activities. These statistics also do not include the material regularly produced for pay cable channels, such as HBO, Showtime, and other purveyors of pornography.

How did this change occur? The country was told in the 1960s that pornography was essentially harmless and that if we just permitted it, people would quickly become bored, and it would all go away. Obviously they were wrong, and now it seems quite impossible to put the genie back in the bottle. A full one-third of the men surveyed at a 1996 Promise Keepers conference said they struggled with pornography.[3] One out of three. How did we get where we are? Through compromise. It happened slowly, one step at a time.

Playboy magazine came out in 1953 with Marilyn Monroe clothed on the cover and undressed on the inside. The pictures of her on the inside were no more revealing than many of the nude images Christian teens see regularly in movies, such as *Titanic*. Pornography in 1953 is PG-13 today and, at the rate we're going, will soon be common on network television. The culture tolerated *Playboy* in 1953. Now we have reaped the harvest of that decision.

But as with the culture, so it is with people. When we cast aside God's Word for ourselves and our children, we send them down the same path. The law of diminishing returns kicks in. Boys, when excited by the nudity in *Titanic* or by the strip-club scene in Disney's *Armageddon*, have found a thrill. They will want to see more. As they get older, it will be R-rated sex scenes, then pornography, then who knows? God's standard is mental and moral purity. Amazingly, many Christian parents lead their children off the path of purity for the sake of a little amusement. Rationalizations abound: "Well, that's the real world. They're going to have to get used to it sometime." The Bible replies, "[I]t is inevitable that stumbling blocks come; but woe to that man through whom the stumbling block comes!" May it not be through us.

I have come to the conclusion that we have dismally failed our children. We have failed our neighbors' children. It is time to take on the issue of immoral entertainment with energy and vigor. There is a scene in the film *Indian in the Cupboard* (a charming film marred by expletives in order to get a PG rating) in which a cowboy and an Indian—magically drawn from the last century into our own—are watching an MTV-style television show with two modern-day boys. As in most rock videos, there are provocatively dressed women dancing in sexually suggestive ways. The cowboy, a worldly fellow, asks the boys, "Do your parents *let* you watch this?"

"Sure," says one of the boys, "it's not real." The cowboy stares at the image on the screen once again. "It's real, son. It's real."

A *Titanic*
Struggle

$\mathint$ ometimes a movie is so good, so right in its understanding
of things human and spiritual, that it seems almost as if
the angels had a hand in it. *Ben-Hur* is such a movie. Never
has the Lord Jesus Christ had a more beautiful cinematic portrayal than in this 1959 epic Hollywood movie. The visual
images, music, and story all combine to present Christ as God
in the flesh, who came into the world to save sinners. And
director William Wyler achieved this without ever showing
the face of Christ. Artistically and dramatically the film succeeded on every level. *Ben- Hur* held the record for winning
the most Oscars until the 1997 Academy Awards.

A more recent example of spiritual and artistic excellence is 1980's *Chariots of Fire*. Christians were delighted that

a major studio film should so completely capture the essence
of what it means to live for Christ. Eric Liddell, a forgotten
Christian hero, spoke again to a new generation. At the
Motion Picture Academy Library, I read with amazement the
original draft of the script for *Chariots of Fire*, for in its original conception, it was a completely different movie! The focus was supposed to be on the professionalization of amateur
sports. As the film turned out, the spiritual themes pushed
that idea into the background. The original script had little
of the spiritual emphasis of the final product, and it even had
a bizarre scene about controlling nocturnal emissions.

How the movie changed into what it became is a mystery to me. One interesting story came from actor Ian
Charleson, who played Eric Liddell. In one scene he was supposed to give an evangelistic sermon after a track meet. The
shooting schedule didn't allow him to learn his lines, so he
placed them in his hat. As the filming began, it started to
rain. His speech was washed out, so he made up the invitation to follow Christ right on the spot. It's a wonderful moment in the film. Again, the Lord allowed this production to
be honored with an unexpected "Best Picture" Oscar that
year. Perhaps the angels *were* involved.

But if angels are involved in Hollywood, it seems more
truly the domain of evil spirits. Hollywood's power to influence people would certainly attract the master tempter, who
makes sin lovely and who masterfully uses film to trap the
weak with lies and images aimed at the flesh.

One of the most remarkable recent films is the megahit
Titanic. It is remarkable for its craftsmanship, its position as
the most expensive movie ever made, and its enormous fi-

nancial success. Because *Titanic* succeeds (for the most part) as entertainment and has been hugely popular with Christians, I have chosen to use this film as a case study for our examination of worldly amusements. To this one movie, I will apply all the principles we have discussed so far. Morally speaking, *Titanic* is no worse than most of Hollywood's creations, but its unique popularity makes it a perfect subject for analysis. Remember the simple two-point definition of a worldly amusement: evil message, evil methods. A worldly amusement is an immoral use of the dramatic or cinematic arts. In order to highlight the spiritual battle behind our moral discussion, I'd like to begin with a little drama of my own.

Let us contemplate (with a tip of the hat to C. S. Lewis and his *Screwtape Letters*) what a conversation might be like among those fallen angels in hell who specialize in temptation. Imagine Pompeius, Underworld Lord of the Arts, making his way along cubicles of laboring demons who are busily devising evils. He passes by the demon in charge of the National Endowment for the Arts and looks in on the latest blasphemy or perversion up for a government grant. He moves on past the music department—a large collective—planning Madonna's next world tour. But Pompeius is most anxious to see the work of Claptrap, a leading darkness in the Hollywood division. He approaches the demon at work over a large drawing table:

> *Pomp:* I say, what is that you're working on Claptrap, a ship?
>
> *Clap:* Yes, my lord. It's one of my finest works yet—a film project.

Pomp: Looks . . . innocent enough.

Clap: Precisely, my lord.

Pomp: What is it?

Clap: The *Titanic.*

Pomp: The *Titanic?* What are you doing with this? Don't forget, your job is to corrupt souls. The last time Hollywood made a movie about the *Titanic,* it was all full of regrets for moral failures and self-sacrifice. Good heavens, they even reenacted that awful singing of a hymn before the ship went down. Most distasteful! It almost suggested—*ugh!*—redemption! A terrible moment. Makes me shudder.

Clap: My lord must know, this one will be different.

Pomp: Oh?

Clap: Yes. The true story is only a backdrop. Hymn singing will be deemphasized. In this movie; only hypocrites among the filthy rich will go to church. I am not bound by history in any meaningful sense. You see, it is the fictional elements I've been working on.

Pomp: Fiction? Now I *am* interested.

Clap: You will not be disappointed. I have brought all the elements together. This will be the most expensive movie ever made—a prestige picture, as the vermin say. The event itself is ready-made to draw an audience: separated families, death, pathos, the unsinkable Molly Brown.

Pomp: Yes, yes. But, what have you added?

Clap: Lovers, my lord. Young lovers—beautiful people.

Pomp: Go on . . .

Clap: Well, the hero is what the humans call "a heartthrob"—handsome, energetic, a free spirit, and . . . an artist.

Pomp: An artist! You must have him do some nude portraits.

Clap: Oh, my lord. I can't ever surprise you. The heroine will be his subject—young woman, most attractive.

Pomp: Exposed flesh. Brilliant. That will feed the young men—

Clap: And boys. A certain percentage, transfixed by this image of the girl, will be locked forever in a cycle of sensual pursuits, craving always a fresh glimpse of flesh, never satisfied.

Pomp: [*Moved to tears*] Delightful (*sniff*). You bring tears to my eyes, Claptrap.

Clap: There is more. The film is really aimed at the girls. We will have them weeping at several points. We will pull every heartstring. They will be emotionally vulnerable. This relationship will be a fantasy model of true love.

Pomp: And you will include . . . ?

Clap: Of course. The lovers will fornicate within days of knowing each other.

Pomp: Excellent. No guilt? No consequences? No marriage?

Clap: No, my lord. And no judgment.

Pomp: No judgment?

Clap: We will move beyond the realm of history. The arrogance of the writers will take us into the afterlife.

Pomp: Eternity? Surely our lovers will suffer the consequences of—

Clap: No consequences, no Enemy Above, no judgment.

Pomp: This will horrify the Christians. You've gone too
far, Claptrap. You can tease their flesh, but attacking
their doctrine will put them on alert.

Clap: It will not horrify them; it will move them to tears.
Think of all we have accomplished in the last twenty
years. They are much weaker than you think.

Pomp: If you're right, it is true genius.

Clap: That's not all, my lord.

Pomp: More?

Clap: The humans, under their own rules, will rate this
film PG-13.

Pomp: Oh, my! Family entertainment!

Clap: So they will believe.

Pomp: That may be the master stroke. Your R-rated efforts have been delightful, but the range is regretfully
too limited.

Clap: We have recognized the problem. PG-13 is our main
focus now.

Pomp: That means reaching into the souls of the churchgoing brats.

Clap: We calculate that the nude scene alone will lower
natural inhibition and shame consciousness several
points, especially in children. The girls will be made
significantly more susceptible to sexual encounters
later, all in the name of love. We have plans for a few
teens to lose their virginity on the way home from
the movie. And just wait until it's out on video. Liv-
ing-rooms are even better than parked cars.

Pomp: And their parents will approve of these early successes, bending little souls our way. Not only approve,
they will pay for the endeavor.

Clap: Our plans rely on their financial resources, my lord.
The enemy blesses his own.

Pomp: Claptrap, I must find a way to reward you.

Clap: My reward is victory. But I have not told you all.
The success of the adventure will be far reaching.
Money drives everything, as you know. They condemn
the rich but will do anything to be like them. Other
studios will see the box-office results and insist on
adding similar content to their films. You know how
unoriginal they are. I will help guide them.

Pomp: I know a few Christian actresses we can pressure
to cave in and reveal a bit of flesh too. Soon they
must give in or leave Hollywood. We win either way.

Clap: They will have to, eventually. And again, the financial incentive will be provided by the church of the
enemy. Damned fools! It's a wonder they don't join us
outright. It's a wonder the enemy doesn't smite them.

Pomp: Yes. It's that grace concept, you know. Let Him love
them and see how much they go His way. Grace, *blah!*

Clap: It may take them to the enemy's presence, but we
can rob them of their power. They have no idea how
serious the Crucified One is about a pure heart. Every year they are more like us. The next generation—

Pomp: Will be more ours than theirs. Show me some more
film ideas.

This little hellish vignette is based on a simple premise:
Satan wages war for our thoughts, our hearts, our affections.

He despises the pure heart Jesus cherishes. Answer the following questions for yourself. If you were Satan, and you wanted to lead souls off in your direction—to deceive them to believe what is false and cherish what is impure—would you make the lie attractive or ugly? Would you make the lie something that appealed to many people or to just a few? Would you make the lie glamorous or seedy? Would you see to it that the world honored it and gave it awards, or would you have the world despise it? Think about it for a moment, and you will see that *Titanic* is a true masterpiece of evil. Its excellence in certain areas actually serves a diabolical purpose.

Evil Methods in *Titanic*?

Let's add some details to the themes brought up by Pompeius and Claptrap. First, the evil methods. The nudity in *Titanic* is designed to inspire lust in normal, healthy males. That's what it is there for. Young men are especially vulnerable to its wiles, for here they see something they are not ordinarily permitted to see. They are allowed a peep through the keyhole. As one Christian teen said to his friend after seeing the movie, "It kind of makes you want to go to art school, huh?" Married men are not immune to this either, as many of them will attest.

Men are not made of steel. We are flesh. Our eyes, like King David's, cause us trouble. Seeing a woman exposed, shamefully exposed in this case, does things to us, both chemically and spiritually. For young men trying to remain pure, such scenes awaken desires. And it is a natural process (in a fallen world) for these awakened desires to play on the mind. The sexual nature, unfairly awakened by images, seeks satisfaction.

I am not saying such images turn a young man into a ravenous beast overnight. It is more subtle than that. It creeps in unawares. Eventually, when the young man is dating, and these desires have already been kindled and fueled by images of other women—images forbidden by Scripture—he finds himself compromising in what he allows his heart to desire. He not only compromises himself, but he also begins, bit by bit, to compromise his date's purity. He manipulates her to gain sexual favors. He becomes a user. This progression is not all directly caused by the immodest images in the movies, but those images feed this corrupt part of his nature. Lust, held in the heart, eventually finds an outlet somewhere. James tells us:

> But each one is tempted when he is carried away and enticed by his own lust. Then when lust has conceived, it gives birth to sin; and when sin is accomplished, it brings forth death. (James 1:14–15)

Immodest images attach themselves to the part of a man that lusts. All kinds of sophisticated talk about art and good taste does not change that simple fact.

Some Christians object that the nudity in *Titanic* is in the context of artwork. Somehow this legitimizes it. This argument in defense of the live nude in film is hopelessly naive. It recklessly disregards Scripture. Let's consider just how many men actually see such art. Film reviewer Darren Leon, in his review of *Titanic*, wrote, "In *Titanic* we get the sexiest sexless scene in the movies—Jack doing a nude portrait of Rose." The "sexiest sexless scene"? Why not call it

the artiest art scene? There is no sexual activity in this sequence. How can a scene be sexy without sex? Simple: Darren
Leon is a man. And he has eyes.

More evidence can be found surfing the Internet's numerous web sites devoted to *Titanic* actress Kate Winslett. One
can even visit the "Kate Winslett Worship Center" and read
comments from her many fans. One contribution (that was
not too obscene) by a Winslett admirer, carried a common
sentiment:

> She is so hot and I love her. She is beautiful. Every fea-
> ture. Weight, curves, face. Everything. She is also great
> for the part and I loved the nude scene!

This is not only lust, it is idolatry. But clearly the nudity is
fueling this idolatry. And of course, this is exactly the reaction intended by the filmmakers. It is designed to be sexually
arousing, and that is sin.

Evil Messages in *Titanic*?

Of course, arousing lust—the use of evil means—is only
one issue. A worldly amusement may also have an evil message. *Titanic* abounds in evil messages through the uncorrected
attitudes, words, and deeds of its heroes. Arrogance, disrespect,
mean-spiritedness, foul speech, and shamelessness are presented
as virtues. In keeping with the emphasis of this book, let's take
a look at the messages of *Titanic* regarding sexuality.

MESSAGE ONE

The first message is that modesty doesn't matter. Rose is
shameless and poses nude as an act of rebellion, which in

fact, it is. This is an attack on shame consciousness, which is God given. Nude scenes, however nonsexual, teach that modesty is not important.

Put yourself in the mind of a child who first sees something like this in a movie. At first the child is shocked, embarrassed, and feels uncomfortable. The theater has a strange quiet. He looks around: no one is leaving; no one is disturbed. *My family isn't offended*, he determines. *I guess it's OK.* Before his eyes is a pretty lady alone with a young man, and she's naked—right there in a movie. He understands she is famous. Later he notices her picture on magazine covers at the checkout line. She's interviewed on TV. She gets lots of money for doing this.

The next time the child sees such a scene, it is not so shocking; it's even . . . interesting, in a funny kind of way. Twenty or thirty movies later, not only is it not shocking, but it is also looked forward to. The enjoyment is not voiced; it is a pleasure hidden quietly in the heart. Gradually the sense of shame is diminished to the point where more and more explicit content is accepted, even sought. Now the child is sophisticated in the eyes of the world. Another term for it is *worldly wise*. He is no longer innocent. The world calls this a good thing, but God weeps at it.

It is only logical that when the rich, the famous, and the beautiful people display themselves without shame, some inner part of those who routinely see this, comes to believe it is not wrong. God and His Word are crowded out of the heart, rejected by lessons learned during a recreational exposure to forbidden images.

MESSAGE TWO

The second message is about fornication. This sin receives hardy and sentimental approval in *Titanic*. Sex is shown as the natural expression of strong feelings, even though the characters barely know each other.

Christians who are asked why they believe *Titanic* is such a great movie say it is a great love story. Many teenage girls have seen the film ten or twenty times. There is a strong emotional reaction to the film. The mediocre sound track sold like crazy, not because the music was superior, but because the music reconnected the hearer to the emotion of the film. "This is the part where . . .," a listener will say, or "You had to see the movie to understand." Remarkably, one version of the film's theme song—aired time and again on the radio—included a few clips of dialogue from the movie. Of course, one of those clips was Rose telling Jack she wanted him to paint her "like you do your Paris girls . . ."—with nothing on. Obviously, the music marketers know full well that this "artistic" nudity is at the core of the sexual relationship.

The emotional connection of a girl to a love story that glorifies fornication is as dangerous to the soul as lust is for a man. The satanic ideal is to attack through the man's eyes and through the woman's emotions. It is interesting to notice how the sexes differ in understanding this about each other. In an otherwise excellent commentary in the June 6, 1998, edition of *World* magazine, Janie Cheany described well how Hollywood uses warm lighting , romantic music, and the soft focus to make fornication seem glorious. She said, "The nudity that earned the film its PG-13 rating is not the main problem." For her, the problem was the romanticized sex scene in the backseat of a car. That scene contained no nudity. But remember what reviewer Darren Leon called the sexiest sexless scene in the movies?—the painting scene with the nudity. Men are not really turned on by love scenes where you can't see anything. They find those scenes tedious at best. But a nude scene without romance? That's the spot to which many boys will wind the family's copy of *Titanic* when Mom is out shopping for an hour. Nudity probably is not the main problem for women. It is the main problem for men. Boys and girls are different. Satan wants them both.

From the tempter's point of view, the love story makes the girls more receptive to the advances of their boyfriends. Of course, *Titanic* is not a love story at all if love is defined biblically. It is the story of an intense erotic attachment. The "love story" is about licentious freedom. It feeds on the teenager's feeling of being trapped by parents and rules and God. Rose, *Titanic*'s heroine, is oppressed by her wicked social class; her greedy, shallow mother; and her cartoonish villain of a fiancé. Her situation is an exaggerated fiction designed to connect with the way many teens *feel*.

Rose is rescued from the monsters who rule over her by a girlishly handsome, free-spirited artist who really "loves" her. He teaches her to soar, to be free. She breaks her society's rules by slumming—hanging around with the poor. Of course, in this movie she is accepted completely. (Director Cameron has no sense of ambiguity about any of this. Real-life rich girls who go slumming are looked down on by the poor, who know that these women can step back into their world of privilege at any time.) She breaks God's rules with eagerness by being rude, posing nude, and having sex in the backseat of a car. Since Jack has freed her, what else can she do but covet him and give herself to him sexually?

The relationship lasts less than seventy-two hours, yet it is the joy of Rose's heart until she is a hundred years old. This extremely brief relationship becomes a bond that stretches across a lifetime. This is pretty sappy stuff, truth be told. Upon reflection, it just doesn't ring true. This will keep *Titanic* off the list of great films in future years, but it has already done its work on one generation of young girls. The big lie has been wrapped up in a beautiful package and delivered right to the target audience: above truth, goodness, purity, or even common courtesy, strong feelings should be your guide.

MESSAGE THREE

At the end of her long life, Rose visits the site of the tragic sinking. There, she dies, but the story does not end. It goes on to the third evil message of *Titanic*: no judgment.

Titanic is the only historical film I can recall which dares to tell what happens to people after they die. Significantly, our fornicators face no judgment—only a godless reunion in a *Titanic* paradise. At this point, director Cameron becomes the judge of the living and the dead. He decides who is excluded. Naturally, the profane fornicators are included. Scripture says:

> Let marriage be held in honor among all, and let the marriage bed be undefiled, for fornicators and adulterers God will judge. (Heb. 13:4)

This fact is categorically denied by *Titanic*. It is not a question of repentance or mercy. The heroes in *Titanic* seek no mercy. They pray no prayers. God is only a swear word to Jack, the hero.

Historically, it is said that on the day the RMS *Titanic* put out to sea, some people were overheard saying, "Even God couldn't sink this ship." The ship represented the pride of human accomplishment, the triumph of human reason. The movie poster for *Titanic* speaks with similar arrogance: "Nothing could keep them apart." This is a strange line for this particular love story, for one of them dies in the disaster. Surely that would keep them apart! It might as well read, "Even God couldn't keep them apart." The moral law, which our heroes violated with impunity, is a "nothing." God, the judge of all, is nothing. It seems fitting that while human arrogance in 1912 was expressed in terms of technology, in the 1990s it is expressed in terms of sexual passion: no one can get in the way of passion—it is all that matters. After the film was out a few months, the line in advertisements was altered to say, "Nothing on earth could keep them apart." This curious change seemed to emphasize, even more, the reunion of Jack and Rose in a paradise without God.

Message Received

Our demon Claptrap assured his Lord Pompeius that Christians would accept not only the nudity, the filthy language, and implied sex (the evil methods), but also the evil messages. I tested this claim by reading comments left at "Christian Spotlight at the Movies," a web site sponsored by Eden Communications/Films for Christ, which has movie reviews, including one of *Titanic*. Following the review, Christians who had seen the film were invited to add their own comments. A few believers stood up for biblical standards. Some were plainly in a state of moral confusion. Others found all sorts of justification for their enjoyment and patronage of *Titanic,* even though they agreed its content was evil. A few examples will demonstrate the problems Christians are having with worldly amusements.

But first, let us remind ourselves once again what the Bible's standard is. The Bible teaches that nakedness outside the bond of marriage is shameful. It teaches absolute purity of mind as well as body. It teaches absolute modesty, as well. It says it is shameful even to speak of the sensual things done in secret by sinners. It commands us not to participate in the unfruitful deeds of darkness. So how do Christians rationalize their participation in worldly amusements? They must either invent their own standard or adopt the world's. Here, in their own words, are some of the ways they do this.

The Age Standard

The "age standard" is what the MPAA does with its movie ratings. It determines that certain things, such as nudity, sex, gore, and bad words are unacceptable for certain ages. But as you grow up, you can see . . . well, anything. These ratings are designed to alert parents that a movie contains material that may not be "suitable" for a child. Most Christians who loved *Titanic* made sure everyone understood that this film was not for small children.

> This was a very well-made movie. The special effects and scenery were outstanding. I was rather shocked at the nudity portrayed in the movie but that's Hollywood for you.

The fact that the story starts in present-day times is a very ingenious idea. I thought that it added much more to the movie. This is an excellent film that seemingly well portrays the emotions of those on the ship. I am sorry to say that the nudity contained in it is offensive and would certainly not be appropriate for anyone under thirteen at least. As for film-making quality, I give this a thumbs up. —T. B.

This is a classic statement of the age standard. T. B. believes it is all right for him to see nudity that is "offensive" and that "shocked" him. His statement even suggests that sixteen-year-old boys could be permitted this shocking and offensive experience.

Another statement:

Easily the best movie that I have seen in years. While I agree that the nudity and the sex scene were not integral to the plot, you need to keep in mind that this movie was made for adults. If you took your children to see a movie that was rated PG-13, it is your fault, not the director's, if you were offended by what you saw. I have an eight year old son that wanted to see this movie. I told him I would see it first and then I would decide. I saw it, I loved it, but I will not allow him to see it. —K. A.

Clearly, K. A. is concerned with the content of the movie itself. She rushes to defend director Cameron's shameless use of actress Kate Winslett. She believes the movie was made for adults. Of course, this is factually incorrect. Jack and Rose's tryst in the backseat of a car was shot as an R-rated scene. It was toned down to win the PG-13 rating sought by all big movies today in order to include children. Be that as it may, she has adopted the age standard, which says, "Evil is OK if you're old enough and you love it"—a standard the Bible does not recognize.

A sixteen-year-old girl wrote:

> This movie is very intense and real. I think adults and mature teens (not kids!) will enjoy it. There is everything in this film: a beautiful love story, spectacular effects, powerful acting, etc. Bring a hankie and enjoy one of the best movies of the year!

She points to the maturity of the viewer as making the film acceptable for a follower of Christ to enjoy. Unfortunately, the "everything" the film has does not include morality. The most important thing does not count as even a something.

A fourteen-year-old adds her wisdom:

> About what age groups this film is appropriate for, it depends on what your standards are. This movie isn't nearly bad enough to be rated R, but when I was thirteen, I wouldn't have been interested in it, not because of the language or nudity, but because the story line would have been boring. I am definitely going to get this when it comes out on video. —H. S.

This fourteen year old nails the issue down for all of us. She says it "depends on what your standards are." She is exactly right, but she stops too soon. What are the standards? Where do we get them? The world says the standard revolves around age alone. After a certain age there are no limits. Is this a

standard Christians should adopt? Since Job had many children when his affliction came upon him, I assume he was
over thirteen when he was following the covenant he made
with his eyes not to gaze at a woman (Job 31:1). Biblical
teaching about men's eyes and modesty does not seem age
restrictive in any way. This girl's standard is "Did I enjoy the
movie at my age?" But how far should this be taken? The age
standard is not only unbiblical, but also entirely subjective.

The adoption of the rating system as a moral standard is
not the intended use of the system. It was meant to be an aid
to parents at a time when movies were showing and saying
things they never had shown before. A Christian should look
at the age standard and ask, "What have they put in here that
may be an offense to my Lord?" Is it really OK, for example, for
an adult Christian to see two people having sex in an R-rated
movie? I would say it depends on what your standards are.

The Me Standard

This standard bases right and wrong on whether or not it
"affects me." This puts nudity and sex, as entertainment, in
the realm of "gray areas"—like eating meat offered to idols,
which may offend some believers but not others. These people
would claim that Job's covenant with his eyes is listed, not as
a standard of righteousness, like the rest of Job 31, but only
because Job had a problem in this area.

One Christian woman wrote,

> I truly enjoyed this movie. I have been a Christian for
> 22 years and I was not offended in the least bit. I agree
> that they could have left out the sexual scene, but I don't

feel there was pornography presented in this movie. . . .
Excellent! The acting, and the effects were awesome!
—K. M., age 28

K. M.'s having been in relationship with Christ for twenty-two years, along with the fact that she was not offended by *Titanic* in the least bit, is given as evidence that nothing was wrong with the film. Her moral standard is based on how she feels about her spiritual life and how she perceives things. No appeal is made to any objective standard. She does not venture to guess what Jesus might think of this film. She is the judge.

The "me standard" fails because Christians have been commanded to live by a different standard—God's Word—which teaches clear principles about things like public displays of nudity, sex acts, and evil messages. Also, the Bible is clear that the human heart is "deceitful above all else" (Jer. 17:9). If we are self-deceived, how can we justify using ourselves as a standard?

The Too-Bad Standard

This is the standard held by Christians who go to see and support worldly amusements, but then say something like "it's too bad they put that in there." This idea is really a variation of the "me standard," but it does acknowledge that there's something wrong with entertainments that assault decency and purity.

One gentleman wrote:

Titanic is a "must see" movie, if there ever is to be one in the '90s. . . . The movie does have at least one use of the

"F word," some nudity, and suggestive scenes of one illicit night at love making. But the rest of the story is so compelling and thought provoking that I can honestly and in good conscience recommend this movie for most adult Christians. —D. S., age 53

This man is looking for the right balance of worthy and unworthy elements.

Another comment:

The most pleasant surprise about this film was that the three-hour, twenty-five-minute running time went by quickly. *Titanic* has a fairly well-written love story that keeps your attention for the first third of the film, so that the iceberg scene actually comes a surprise. The production design and special effects are magnificent and transport you believably to the world of 1912. However, the film does have unnecessary profanity, nudity, and the glorification of immoral behavior and could easily have been written on the PG level. Yet, all in all, I would strongly recommend the film. —K. B., age 26

K. B. accurately diagnosis *Titanic*'s moral failures, but he would still "strongly recommend" this film.

The problem with the "too-bad standard" is that it reduces things like the "glorification of immoral behavior," to the level of breaking one's favorite coffee mug. "Oh! Too bad!" What is meant by *bad*? K. B. understands the bad to be moral evil, but he cannot do other than recommend this glorification of evil, because the movie is a magnificent example of special effects and set design. Again the question is not asked, Does God care more about production design, special effects, and thrills, or the glorification of immoral behavior? If it is the latter, should not the Christian tune his or her heart to the cares of the Lord? Indeed, if *sin is glorified,* then the excellence of the effects and design serve only satanic ends! Does high-quality presentation of evil make the message less evil? I would think it would make the evil message worse by adding to the attractiveness of sin. But somehow K. B. can't see this.

The Cover-My-Eyes Standard

This is the most amusing of all the rationalization standards. It has such a childlike quality. One immediately becomes curious and wonders if those who "cover their eyes," ever peek! Here's a real classic:

> Even though I understand the concerns of parents over the nude scene in this film, I still don't believe that that was enough to discredit the beauty of this film. Nor would I call it pornography. When I was a child and we saw films with nude scenes and sex scenes in them, my mother applied a practice that I still use at 25 years of age . . . *she covered my eyes.* And I still cover my eyes. —C. U., age 25

Imagine a twenty-five year old man having the moral sense to cover his eyes in a movie theater, but at the same time not seeing anything wrong with financially supporting the whole corrupt endeavor from which he must shield himself. This young man demonstrates how far Christians will go to be as close to the world as possible. One imagines an early Christian who, at the gladiator shows, loves to see a good fight but who closes his eyes as the death blow is struck. What a victory for Christ!

The Confused

Some viewpoints expressed about *Titanic* are difficult to label. These are "the confused." The movie has touched them emotionally, so they labor to call it "good," even though they know it is evil.

> I found the "sketch scene" to be done in remarkably good taste. Jack's perspective was that of an artistic point of view. It was plainly obvious that Jack didn't see her in a sexual way, instead he was very intent on his artwork, and the beauty of his subject. The older Rose held his behavior in high regard, referring to him as a gentleman and chiding those who thought the event was something base. Although the character of Rose was shown nude fairly briefly, I didn't find this scene in any way arousing. I saw a young man of good character drawing a beautiful woman, much the way he would a beautiful sunset . . . As a Christian, of course, I can't condone their behavior in the car, and I really don't think the scene was needed . . . —M. S., age 25

As children do, M. S. tries very hard to make the hero virtuous. Jack paints Rose nude, but he doesn't lust. He is a man of "good character." This same man is copulating with this same woman only a few hours later, and of course, we can't condone *that*, but still we are to believe he didn't see her in a sexual way? Confusion. This confusion is common and highlights the danger of worldly amusements and is why the church has condemned such entertainment since the early centuries.

Another example:

> One of the major underlying themes of this movie was of sacrificial love. Watch as the character Jack Dawson always puts everything on the line all the time, always sacrificing himself for the good of others. —J. R., age 20

Jack, a fictional hero, *always* sacrifices himself for the good of others? The Bible regards self- sacrifice as a virtue, but the use of the word "always" here is revealing. Jack could not control his sexual urges for even two days on Rose's behalf. He was not interested in her purity or her future. He took advantage of her at an extremely weak moment in her life. But the film's emotional impact has reshaped this Christian's standard of righteousness. Again, notice how hard J. R. labors to make Jack all good. He can't see that the fictional Jack's goodness in some areas is used to proclaim his immorality as good too.

Jack being fictional makes a big difference in another important way. Many of the truly sacrificial and noble individuals on the real RMS *Titanic* were slandered and skewered by Cameron's perverse rewrite of history. He gave all the virtue to his fornicating teen, and literally stole it from real men and women who deserve to be remembered better. But the movie touched emotions, and in current popular culture, emotions are truth.

Certainly *Titanic's* greatest blasphemy is the afterlife sequence. But not all Christians detected the obvious message of the film's conclusion:

> I was very moved by the final scene in *Titanic*, in which Rose apparently enters into Paradise. There were no class or social distinctions there, only radiance and love. It was also interesting to note who was and who was not there. God alone will truly be the judge on that final day. And I prefer to leave the judgment to Him! —L. C., age 39

The suggestion here is that we cannot judge. Only God is judge. But *Titanic* places James Cameron precisely in the position of God, a role Cameron seems to have taken a shine to. He determined who entered Paradise and who did not. He determined that hypocrites are out and fornicators are in, based on his own prejudices and favored sins. But L. C., because she enjoyed the film, can't see past her own feelings. This New Age paradise found a home in at least one Christian's heart.

Final Thoughts

How can Christians in such great numbers overthrow a biblical standard for the world's or their own? One reason is the power of art to seize a place in the heart. I used to believe that Pascal went too far when he wrote that among all those amusements invented by the world "there is none more to be feared than the theater." But to see professed followers of Jesus gravitate toward anything that amuses them or thrills them or makes them cry *is* frightening.

Another reason, I suppose, is the simple fact that we have become jaded by the pounding we have taken from our culture. It is nearly impossible to escape. While watching the 1998 Super Bowl with a group of guys from church, an advertisement came on for the movie *The Mask of Zorro*. The commercial showed Zorro slicing away a woman's clothing with his sword until she was topless. My eight-year-old son saw it and cried out, "No! No! Where's the *old* Zorro?" He wanted Zorro to be virtuous. A small victory in my house? Perhaps. If so, it is because such content is never permitted in our viewing choices. My children know the standard. But I can't erase that image from his mind. The continuous pounding of such images hammers away our resistance until the twisted looks straight, the unclean doesn't look dirty, the immoral no longer feels wrong.

Another reason is that the church has grown silent. Many pulpits no longer preach that we must not love the world, nor serve two masters and that we must, instead, take every thought captive to the obedience of Christ. The desire not to offend anyone in our services pushes such messages to the back alleys of the church—words for the faithful minority to discover on their own. The standard is not taught, so the world or the deceived heart takes over the role of judge.

Untaught Christians lack discernment. They go to the world for advice. Many Christians act as though the rating system came down from heaven. They do not see it as something created and used by the world for its own purposes. Some Christians believe that *Titanic*'s PG-13 rating makes the film morally suitable for children. They don't understand the "rating game"—the subject of our next chapter.

The
Rating Game

Many parents were a little shocked when, near the beginning of the delightful movie *E.T.: The Extraterrestrial*, the young child Eliot utters an obscenity at the dining table, which seemed strangely out of place. Why put such a word in a movie so obviously aimed at small children? The answer is found in the rating game.

As it was created, *E. T.: The Extraterrestrial* was not violent enough, sexy enough, or crude enough to get anything more than a G rating. The prospect of a G rating frightened Steven Spielberg, who did not have enough confidence in his movie to let it go into theaters with that label. In his mind, children who were a little older—say, nine or ten— would not desire to see his movie, simply because of the rating. So a word was invented and put into the mouth of the child, to be heard by millions of children each time the video player is engaged.

Spielberg's rational has become the controlling factor in Hollywood's decision-making about film content. Children's movies, except for animated features, are almost always rated PG, which means some element—vulgar language, sexual innuendo, a sex scene, oozing blood, etc.—has been added to the film, requiring parental oversight. Films truly aimed at children are nearly always tainted with vulgar language. Recent films of quality such as *Fly Away Home*, *A Fairy Tale*, and *Indian in the Cupboard* all have the added word or two for the sole purpose of obtaining the PG rating.

There was a time when even adult entertainment could be rated G. The excellent, Academy Award-winning movie *A Man for All Seasons* represents an intelligent, sophisticated form of entertainment that simply would not appeal to children. Yet it contains no offensive elements. It is great art, yet it didn't need to use sheer vulgarity or shamelessness to achieve "adult status."

A Man for All Seasons is rated G because it *can* be viewed by all audiences without causing offense. That was the original intent of the rating service: to inform. But that intent is now a secondary purpose.

Originally, a movie would be made, and a rating applied to the finished product. This was a device to inform people in a general way about the content of the film produced. It wasn't long before ratings began to shape content according to marketability. If a rating was too high (such as an X, or now NC-17), a movie would have a smaller audience or fewer venues in which to play. The film would be altered (at least for domestic release) to get a rating that would allow for the widest distribution possible.

Today, ratings shape content in a new way—in a more sophisticated and cynical way. Films are routinely made with specific ratings in mind, just as Spielberg targeted a specific rating for *E.T.: The Extraterrestrial*. This aiming at a specific rating is based on money and on assumptions about human nature that clearly reveal Hollywood's understanding of its own influence in degrading the culture. Hollywood has trained American tastes, since the 1960s, to expect vulgar language, explicit sexuality, and bloody violence in any film aimed at adults.

The idea of a film for adults that carries a G rating has vanished. Any film made for adults must be reworked with "adult" content, which no longer means "adult" in the sense of "mature," but rather, indicates the presence of material from which parents have traditionally sought to shield children. In fact, these elements have traditionally been considered inappropriate for mixed company (that is, for ladies and gentlemen together). Thus, anyone wishing to see a movie made for grown-ups has been forced to accept that *grown-up* means "all the things polite society once considered inappropriate for any company of decent people."

Sadly, the duplicity of the Hollywood mind-set does not stop there. Children have a desire to see what they are not supposed to see. They want to be like adults, and they long for initiation into the world of adult things. Knowing this, Hollywood plays a game of temptation, carefully crafting the big blockbuster movies each year to be raunchy enough to feed the increasingly jaded tastes of children, yet not so raunchy as to elicit parental disapproval. Getting both parents and children in the theater at full price has become the driving force behind most of what Hollywood does. Christians, therefore, need to understand four things about the movie rating system as it exists today.

Movie Ratings Are Not Based on Biblical Morals

The people who rate movies are not working from a biblical framework. Their perspective is that of the world, not the kingdom of Christ. The world does not recognize any content as inherently evil, only as age inappropriate. By contrast, Christians are to let God's word define evil. Therefore, our concerns and standards must be fundamentally different from those presented to us by the Motion Picture Association of America. The world says that a stripper, completely nude and doing her "act," is appropriate viewing for seventeen-year-old young people and older. Jesus' standard would exclude such viewing by *any* godly individual.

PG-13, a rating created in 1984 as a middle ground between PG and R, says that the following items are acceptable for children over twelve:

- Nudity of a nonsexual nature can be used in PG-13 films. The more oriented the nudity is to sexual acts, the more likely the film is to receive an R.
- Violence that is too extreme or too persistent will get an R rating. PG-13 may have blood, but not too much in the way of sheer gore, unless it is fanciful.
- Multiple expletives are acceptable for PG-13. Only recently, the rule was for "one use of the harsher sexu-

ally derived words." This was to be used as an expletive, and not in a sexually suggestive way. This rule
collapsed in 1997. It was cast aside on the appeal of
Julia Robert's for her film My Best Friend's Wedding.
Originally given an R, the ratings board caved in and
allowed a sexually suggestive use of the F word. Another barrier down. By the time Disney's 1998 Armageddon appeared, its PG-13 rating allowed "two F
words, one F-word derivative, a profane hand ges-
ture, many mild obscenities, many scatological references, many anatomical references."[1]

The words that officially follow the PG-13 rating say,
"Parents strongly cautioned: some material may be inappropriate for children under 13." This is the advice of the world!
Yet, Christian parents routinely take their children to these
films and rarely have a doubt that they, themselves, should
be in attendance. The rating board never considers the Word
of God when it makes its decisions. Christians have a higher
obligation.

Movie Ratings Have Changed in What Is Permitted

Jack Valenti, president of the MPAA and apologist for
all things wicked, stated in a speech broadcast on C-SPAN,
that the ratings system is not an oak, but a willow. The metaphor is enormously helpful. The ratings system is not strong
and inflexible but, rather, bends with the winds of culture.
As the culture accepts more vulgarity, public nudity, and perverse lifestyles, so the rating levels change to allow younger
audiences to experience such things.

For example, *Midnight Cowboy*, an X-rated film in the 1960s, today has been granted an R. The content is the same, but now it almost seems tame. Other extreme films from the era—films such as *Carnal Knowledge*, rated R in 1960s for its frank sexuality—are far surpassed in prurience, language, and sexuality by some PG-13 and even a few PG films of today (as well as by family-hour network television). As morals decline, ratings shift to accommodate and accelerate the decline. The question for believers, of course, concerns biblical standards. Is God's Word an oak or a willow?

Movie Ratings Have a Wide Latitude in Actual Content

I have mentioned how children's films often seek the PG rating through the addition of a four-letter word or two, believing that a G rating is a financial "kiss of death." Yet other PG films are loaded with degrading and perverse content. Mel Gibson's *Maverick* contains numerous vulgar words, lewd jokes, and an explicit and completely pointless sex scene, and it tells us that the main hero and his father have both had sex with the same woman. The film was rated PG.

On the R-rated side, there is the film *Glory*, which contains only a few expletives and two fairly intense battle scenes. Also receiving an R rating is *Starship Troopers*, a film with coed shower scenes, explicit love-making, foul language, and people's brains being sucked out and eaten by giant bugs. For these films, there is no real comparison in content, but they get the same rating. All this is to say that you can't tell much from Hollywood's film ratings, and you can't trust them as reliable guides.

There Is a "PG-13 Crunch"

We have discussed PG-13 at some length, but it must be understood how pervasive this rating will be in the next few years. The megahits—films making over $200 million—carry this rating. *Independence Day* and *Men in Black* convinced studios that this is the rating for which to aim. This is why the 1998 blockbuster *Titanic* labored so hard to keep a money-making PG-13 rating, although pressing the allowable "nonsexual nudity" to the limit. While the purpose was supposedly an "artistic" one—the heroine posing nude for the artist-hero—many reviewers picked up on the sexual energy in the scene. (Remember the reference to it as the "sexiest sexless scene" in the movies?) Indeed, artist and model do become lovers, and of course, the sexual fantasies of many thousands of Christian young people were fed by these images. The rating allowed the studio to reach many families that an R rating would have driven off. This is why the love scene in the back of a car, originally filmed very explicitly, had to be muted in the final version.

An October, 1997 article in the *Los Angeles Times* discussed Hollywood's new love-affair with PG-13. Industry people uniformly profess their economic interest in PG-13. There are twenty-three million children between eight and thirteen years of age. Anything less than a PG-13 rating, they believe, is too tame for children over eight. Amy Pascal, president of Columbia Pictures, is quoted as saying,

> Kids are so much hipper and more sophisticated than they used to be that younger kids want to see stuff that has a little edge to it. [2]

New Line Cinema's Mitch Goldman said the film version of *Lost in Space*, based on the old family-friendly TV show, is carefully tailored to receive a PG-13 rating.

> The script and production are designed to enthrall an 8-year-old and an 18-year-old. It's imperative we get a PG-13 rating.[3]

The result of this, naturally, is that children's films become almost nonexistent. Only 3 percent of 1997 Hollywood releases were rated G. Not only does that leave little product for children, it also means that no film for *the whole family* will be without some vulgar, sexual, or extremely violent elements. Ratings have come to drive content for profit. They no longer simply label what is made.

The example of a Kathleen Kennedy project that failed shows just how lockstep the Hollywood mentality is. Kennedy, one of the most successful producers in Hollywood (*Jurassic Park*; *The Lost World*; *Twister*; *E.T.: The Extraterrestrial*; *Back to the Future*), wanted to make a live action version of E. B. White's *Trumpet of the Swan*. The film would follow the example of the highly successful *Babe*, using advanced technology to make the animal characters "talk." It was a G-rated product, yet she told the *Times*, "I couldn't get it made. The common response was . . . it will only appeal to very young children."[4]

The picture emerging reveals Hollywood to be a very amoral business, seeking the broadest possible audience for each film by finding just the right amount of crude material—enough to appeal to increasingly jaded children, yet not quite enough to drive off parents. And as long as parents believe that the PG-13 rating is harmless, Hollywood will make millions, while each generation becomes more harsh, more crude, and more sexually inflamed.

In a very direct way, the church of Christ Jesus has made this happen. Films with nudity and sexual immorality that are promoted as such, don't do well at the box office. Movies like *Showgirls* or Demi Moore's *Striptease* don't make a lot of money. I believe this is because Christians—a large minority of the population—will not attend such blatant appeals to sexual gratification. But put the same content in an action film, a disaster epic, a comedy, or a weepy, sentimental "woman's" picture, and Christians will accept virtually anything. What we have, then, is worldliness that is a little softer, a little more subtle, with a little more story line. It is a blended product—truly worldly but with some appeal to the more innocent desire for amusement or pathos. By accepting this compromise wholesale, Christians have actively agreed to let slip away a tradition of excellent but decent entertainment—intelligent enough for adults and safe enough for children. We are trapped for the foreseeable future by our own willingness to compromise.

From
the Top

I have labored for many pages now to persuade you that worldly amusements should be shunned by the people of God. I am sure you will not be surprised that people disagree with me. I believe I have the support of Scripture and, until about twenty years ago, of church teaching. The consensus of church opinion has been turned upside down in the last two decades. Evangelical leaders either have grown silent about worldly amusements or have grown fond of them, so that now those embracing the new tide of acceptance dominate all discussion of Hollywood in evangelical circles.

Nearly all the "experts"—and there are not many—hold a view of worldly amusements strongly opposed to the traditional teaching of the church and opposed, I believe, to the simple teaching of the Bible. These individuals are generally found in one of two groups: (1) those directly involved in Hollywood; or (2) those who comment on it. I will address the views of both. A few individuals belong to both groups: notably, Franky Schaeffer, who has written two books about Christianity and the arts, and who is also a professional film-maker. Schaeffer is a man of intense feelings and of some influence, at least in years past. Because of his position, I feel he deserves separate treatment. The two chapters that follow attempt to respond to his work.

Many of the Christian writers on the subject of film, appear to have been influenced by the work of H. R. Rookmaaker, a professor of art history at the Free University of Amsterdam. A mentor to Francis Schaeffer for many years, his writings have been influential. One of Rookmaaker's books bears the title *Art Needs No Justification*. That title has become a dogma, which turns up frequently in Christian articles and books. What does it mean?

The Wicked Pietist

The expression "art needs no justification" primarily is directed at what modern writers call "pietism." They define *pietism* as a Christian lifestyle that excludes any activity not directly expressive of Christian faith. By their definition, a pietist seeing a movie, such as *Good-bye, Mr. Chips*, would ask, "Where's the gospel?" If painting a bowl of fruit, he or she would have to add a Bible verse across the top of the painting to give it a spiritual purpose. The pietist labels anything that is not specifically Christian as "worldly." He does not see creativity as inherently honoring God.

I am not a pietist by this definition. I'm not sure I have even met a person like the one I just described, although I'm sure such folk must exist somewhere. I do believe that if we were to weigh the errors of pietism on the one hand and of worldliness on the other, worldliness would turn out to be a far more common problem, which leads us to a second, not always clearly stated, meaning behind "art needs no justification." This is the idea that art is worthy, even if it is worldly; that is, art is not accountable to moral standards.

K. L. Billingsley is a screenwriter and author. His enjoyable book *The Seductive Image* (1989) expounds both aspects of the idea that art needs no justification. He identifies pietism as legalism. Billingsley's personal manifesto is stated thus:

> With Newton, Pascal, and others, I believe that all truth is God's truth. With Bach, Michelangelo and Cervantes, I believe that art needs no justification. Hence, I believe there is no religious case against the movies, only against the abuse and misuse of them. [1]

Now, I would agree entirely with this last statement, but I suspect that Billingsley and I would define "misuse" in very different ways. This becomes clear as we examine Billingsley's definition of worldliness.

> "Do not conform any longer to the pattern of this world, but be transformed *by the renewing of your mind*," says the relevant biblical text. I take this to mean that one's way of thinking is changed, which leads to this statement in

the same context: "For by the grace given me I say to every one of you: Do not think of yourself more highly than you ought, but rather think of yourself with sober judgment. . . ." Hence, I believe, the essence of worldliness is not a question of abstaining from movies, cards, or dancing. Rather, the essence of worldliness is hubris, holding an inflated view of oneself or exalting oneself above others. Preventing that condition is a much trickier business than refusing to see *Ghostbusters* and chiding those who do.[2]

This is remarkable exegesis. For Billingsley, Romans 12:2 becomes *the* relevant biblical text on worldliness. It has to do with the mind alone, he says. And at this point he becomes intentionally vague. Worldliness is not abstaining from movies (generalized), but worldliness is an inflated view of self. *Ghostbusters*, then—a movie with trashy language, oral sex jokes, explicit sexual banter—is not worldly. Indeed, logically, by Billingsley's definition, *Striptease* would not be a worldly movie either, nor *Boogie Nights*, nor even hard-core porn, because they do not involve an inflated view of the self. Would the apostle agree with this, I wonder? Is Romans 12:2 the only relevant text?

Isn't 1 John 2:15–17 a more complete definition?

Do not love the world, nor the things in the world. If anyone loves the world, the love of the Father is not in him. For all that is in the world, the lust of the flesh, the lust of the eyes and the boastful pride of life, is not from the Father, but is from the world. And the world is pass-

ing away, and also its lusts; but the one who does the will
of God abides forever.

It seems clear that worldliness involves more than an inflated
view of self. John describes things outside the self: things "in
the world" and one's love for those things. It involves the
affections being bestowed on things opposed to God. It involves not only pride, but also covetousness and lust. Certainly many films that Billingsley considers acceptable are
worldly by this definition. *Ghostbusters*, along with the vast
majority of Hollywood's current product, is directed right to
the lust of the flesh, the lust of the eyes, and the boastful
pride of life—all three of which are radically at odds with
the living God. James poses a relevant question:

> Do you not know that friendship with the world is hostil-
> ity toward God?" (James 4:4)

Billingsley asserts the harmlessness of the movies at one
point:

> Myriads of people, young and old, who regularly attend
> movies are relatively unaffected by them. They go to the
> theater, as they would go to a basketball game or concert,
> watch *Bambi* or *Hoosiers*, are entertained, and for the most
> part that's the end of it. To assume that everyone will
> imitate what they see is practically to deny free will, spiri-
> tual discernment, or moral courage.[3]

Though he does not tell us what gauge he has used to
determine the influence of movies on those who attend,

Billingsley's choice of examples is illuminating. To place in our minds a harmless impression of movies, he reaches for *Bambi*, a 1942 cartoon, and *Hoosiers*, one of the few films Christians openly embraced in 1986. I would agree that these films are harmless. However, less than 5 percent of Hollywood's product each year is as harmless as these two! His selection is so unrepresentative, as to be spurious. As I write these words, the local mall is playing eight different features: six are rated R, and the other two—*Titanic* and *Blues Brothers 2000*—are rated PG-13. My guess is that none of these films lack elements that might negatively affect a viewer's morality, yet these theaters are full of Christian patrons—mainly teens—bowing to the theory, whether they know it or not, that "art needs no justification."

Billingsley's suggestion that evil images are easily overthrown by free will, spiritual discernment, and moral courage, ignores all the biblical counsel regarding the use of our eyes and our minds. It denies the power of art. It disregards the cumulative effect of worldly amusements on the soul. Truly, if so much discernment and courage are needed just to see a movie, perhaps these qualities are better exercised beforehand in the process of selecting an evening's recreation.

The disciples of the "art needs no justification" theory cannot contemplate the possibility that the films they love might be worldly. Another comment from Billingsley on the power of cinema is most revealing:

> If well-directed, well-written scenes of great power and beauty exalt the viewer, as everyone admits, it surely follows that poorly-written, poorly directed scenes of squa-

lor and depravity will to some degree degrade the viewer. How can it be otherwise?[4]

Once again, Billingsley's sidestepping choice of alternatives demands close scrutiny. He is right, of course, as far as he goes. But something most needful is missing here. What about the well-written, well-directed scenes of squalor and depravity? What about the award-winning films, such as *Silence of the Lambs* or *The English Patient*, a film praised far-and-wide for its frank sensuality? Uplifting or worldly? A misuse of film or a right use? Billingsley and others are strangely quiet on these questions. But these are the primary questions, whose answers reveal what our standards actually are and where they came from.

Batman Forever-Tarnished

Hollywood is well-populated with Christians. Several have been in positions of some influence. It is a mystery that there are not better projects coming out of Hollywood. Or is it? Does the idea that "art needs no justification" sap the moral courage to fight for more uplifting work? The track record of well-publicized Christians in Hollywood is not encouraging.

I know nothing about Lee and Janet Batchler. I am sure they are nice folks. All I know about them is that they are credited with the story and screenplay for *Batman Forever*. And I know that they have been honored in southern California's Christian arts community as believers who have "made it." What they have made is money and a name for themselves. They have also made a movie—aimed at children—that is worldly, vulgar, and crude. They have made a contribution to our morally polluted environment. They have sent God's children a message from the darkness.

All of the modern Batman movies are silly, full of unbelievable action sequences, and stuffed with expensive sets and special effects. They present a new Batman for the '90s. Old-time fans of Batman were shocked when the first movie came out and made their hero a rather cold- hearted killer. But since old fans are a tiny minority of the moviegoing public, the films were a huge success. The first two movies were also sexually suggestive and contained bad language. The third in the installment—*Batman Forever*—was widely anticipated because it introduced Batman's famous sidekick, Robin—a Robin for the '90s, that is. Also, with Christian writers, one might have expected a shift up from the low moral tone of the two earlier films. In fact, it was a shift down.

I skipped *Batman Forever* when it played in the theater, but I borrowed the video from a friend. I wanted to scrutinize it. As I watched—pen in hand, consciously ignoring all the razzmatazz action sequences (not hard to do)—I observed the film for its overall tone and, specifically, for its presentation of sexuality. Remember, this is a comic book with live people. Nothing compels the direction of the story except the heart of the writer and possibly a hint from the studio to aim for a PG-13 rating.

Now, when I was a child, I read Batman comics and watched the goofy television series (although at the time I thought it was serious). My children are permitted to watch the edgy, but virtuous, Batman of the Animated Series. In all the years Batman has been around, it took Christian writers to put *bastard* and *screw you* in Robin's mouth. The Riddler was always a little crazy, as I recall, but he never before stooped to accuse Robin of being one who "watches Saturday morning cartoons and dreams of being naked with a girl." Who added *that*? And why?

Of course, these are side issues. The heart (however tiny) of *Batman Forever* is the relationship between Batman and Chase Meridian—an expert in multiple-personality disorders. Their relationship actually consists of remarkably few lines of dialogue, and those are simply bizarre. There is no reason given why Batman is even attracted to Chase, except that she's pretty and doesn't sweat, even during vigorous exercise.

The first real conversation takes place on the top of city hall. Chase, fascinated by Batman, lights up the "Bat signal." Batman arrives:

Chase: What is it about the wrong kind of man . . . now, black rubber . . .

Batman: Try firemen.

Chase: [*Throwing back her coat to reveal a lingerie-clad body, cleavage on display*] I'll bring the wine; you bring your scarred psyche.

Batman: Direct, aren't you?

Chase: You like strong women. I've done my homework. Or do I need skintight vinyl and a whip?

Batman: I haven't had much luck with women.

Chase: Maybe you haven't met the right woman. [*They are interrupted.*]

What kind of mind would write a scene like this for a
kid's movie? The second meeting takes place at Chase's office, where Bruce Wayne (Batman) seeks her expertise. He
invites her to a party.

> *Bruce:* I've got to get you out of those clothes.
> *Chase:* Excuse me?
> *Bruce:* And into a black dress.

Their third conversation. He as Bruce Wayne discussing
Chase's pop psychology.

> *Bruce:* We're all two people.
> *Chase:* [*Sensually*] Rage, violence, passion. [*They kiss, but
> are interrupted again.*]

Batman rescues Chase at the party. She kisses him and
whispers, "My place. Midnight." The next scene is in the
Bat Cave.

> *Alfred:* She seems lovely and wise.
> *Batman:* I've never been in love before.
> *Alfred:* Go to her. Tell her how you feel.
> *Batman:* She loves Batman, not Bruce Wayne.

The scene switches to Chase's bedroom at midnight. She
is waiting for Batman to arrive, except . . . Good heavens!
She's not dressed yet. She's not dressed at all. She's waiting
for him in the nude. Covered only with her silk bedsheets,

she greets him at the window. They kiss without a word. She
pulls back.

> *Chase:* I'm sorry. I can't believe this. I've imagined this
> moment since I first saw you. Your eyes, your lips,
> your body. And now I have you, and I'm wishing you
> were someone else.
> I guess a girl has to grow up sometime. I've met
> someone. He's not you. I hope you understand.
> *Batman:* I understand. Well . . . [*He exits.*]

Other than being really stupid, the lesson to children is
clear: lady professionals, loved by the good guys, wait in
the nude for the first date to arrive. They are sexually provocative in the extreme. Sex equals love. The "moral" is
that Chase really only wants sex at the drop of a hat with
the man she loves, not the fantasy figure of Batman. This
qualifies as a worldly definition of love, to say the least. No
one in this movie questions her sanity or virtue. Instead,
we are told she is "lovely and wise." Biblically, of course,
Chase fits exactly the evil woman of Proverbs 6—9. But in
Batman Forever the message is: Good girls do anything for
passion. Good guys go along.

The Batchlers, as writers, had every opportunity to swim
against the tide. They had the opportunity to offer to millions a heroine who was not foul-mouthed, sexually aggressive, and promiscuous. At the very least, they could have
had Batman being turned off by such a woman. But as written, her sexual desirability makes whatever she does good.

To be fair to the Batchlers, maybe none of this material is theirs. Maybe all of it was dropped in from somewhere else. Films do sometimes get reworked by many hands before the final product. But the Batchlers seem to enjoy the prestige of having written this movie. Their own publicity material boasts that *Batman Forever* was the "number-one box-office feature in 1995." To my knowledge, the Batchlers have never publicly disassociated themselves from this shameful movie. If they want the credit, they must also bear the responsibility. How many young minds went home with an image of Chase in her bedsheets? How many girls watched her win Batman's attention by throwing open her clothes? How many heard the reasonable Alfred call this "lovely and wise"? Wouldn't any Christian be ashamed to have a hand in putting such decadence before the American public? Before Jesus' little ones? Rumor has it the Batchlers are working on a film about Stanley and Livingstone. Let's hope David Livingstone, the great crusader for Christ, fairs better at their hands than the Caped Crusader.

Moral Hocus-Pocus

Another prominent Christian in Hollywood is Ralph Winter. He has had a large role in several of the movie incarnations of the old *Star Trek* television series. He is an active and reasonably successful member of the Hollywood community. I have seen the *Star Trek* movies, and found them enjoyable for the most part. Sadly, they are sprinkled with completely unnecessary profanity at times. But even that, at least in one of the films, became a sort of criticism of the late twentieth century's explosion of bad language.

One film Ralph Winter took a lot of credit for was the Walt Disney feature *Hocus Pocus* (1993), a comedic movie about three witches brought back to life to torment a teenage boy. I went to see this movie (rated PG) with my children because it was produced by a Christian for the Walt Disney company. I assumed it would be like the old Disney movies—a harmless diversion at worst, morally uplifting at best. I got a rude shock from Michael Eisner's new Disney.

This "family film" focuses continually on the teenager's virginity, an embarrassing condition since being a virgin is uncool. He likes a pretty girl, but she's not interested. The boy's little sister tells the girl that her brother "likes your yabos"—a crude term for breasts. This "joke" came from nowhere, apparently to show how sexually sophisticated and uninhibited the eight-year-old sister is. She is "with it," not hung up about sex. When the boy's lusts are mentioned on the screen, one might hope for some morally redemptive element—some suggestion that virginity is more than just a handy tool against witches. Such redemption never comes.

Other weird elements are included. On Halloween, the boy's mother goes to a Halloween party dressed as Madonna with a large cone-shaped brassiere and trashy clothes. More humor? It is no surprise that even Leonard Maltin's secular video guide called the film a discredit to Disney family entertainment.

The film was a huge disappointment, but Ralph Winter's appearance on a Christian radio broadcast in southern California was even more depressing. Since the subject was Christians in the arts, I was hoping to hear an explanation or apology from Winter about *Hocus Pocus*. Instead, the program was devoted to ridiculing people with moral standards. Once again, the watchword was "art needs no justification." Winter also claimed that witches' organizations protested *Hocus Pocus* because it portrayed traditional wicked witches. He said he got criticism from Christian groups for making a film with witches in the first place. You can't make everyone happy, he concluded, so why worry? He never addressed the crude humor and sexual elements in his film. It's a family movie, he suggested, just for fun. Some fun.

The Good

Amazingly, the most dare-to-be-different, morally uplifting films—rare as they are—do not come from Christians. The touching *Driving Miss Daisy* came from secular sources. The very worldly Emma Thompson gave us the excellent and very decent *Sense and Sensibility*. Jane Austin fever from that success led to a delightful screen version of *Emma*. The wonderful film *Glory* raised hopes that director Ed Zwick might bring some good, wholesome drama to the screen. Sadly, his later films disappointed that hope. But what about the Christians in Hollywood? Is it lack of talent or lack of nerve that keeps them on a treadmill of mediocrity and worldliness?

The Curious Age of *World* Magazine

We have discussed two failures that have left the church morally confused and easily compromised. First, Christian thinkers on entertainment have failed to uphold biblical principles adhered to for generations by the church. Second, Christians in Hollywood have failed to be salt and light in any discernable way. To these failures we can add a third: the failure of Christian media to provide clear moral guidance. It seems that nearly all Christian media willing to discuss the movies are afraid to condemn even their most blatant excesses. There's an almost palpable fear of being labeled "unsophisticated" or "fundamentalist." This fear of the opinions of others has paralyzed the cultural commentators to which Christians turn for guidance.

For example, *World* magazine, in a February 1998 review of *The Gingerbread Man*, mildly criticized the R-rated thriller for going after suspense too much and for not emphasizing the "excellent morality tale" in the story. The moral was that the protagonist wouldn't be in trouble if he hadn't spent the night with a woman he met at a party. Other than these faults, the reviewer concluded that *The Gingerbread Man* is "a good movie that could have been great." Nothing is mentioned in this review about *how* this morality tale was told.

An examination of secular sources reveals that *The Gingerbread Man* contains "casual obscenities, nudity and sex play, and realistic violence." Secular reviewers are often careful to describe content that would be offensive to people with traditional moral sensibilities. *World* didn't bother, and seldom does. Apparently, *World* did not consider these elements to be standing in the way of the movie's greatness, criticizing only its failure to emphasize the message strongly enough. *World*'s review of *Great Expectations* (1998) again failed even to suggest any problem with the explicit nudity and sexual scenes in the film (*World*, Feb. 7, 1998). In the moral view of *World* magazine—which aspires to be a Christian publication along the lines of *Time* or *Newsweek*—none of this exposed flesh, shameful behavior, or filthy language is called inappropriate for Christian amusement. The reviewer's major complaint is that the film didn't follow the novel. It must be noted, however, that while *World*'s review does not warn about the shameful content, a tiny box does say the film is rated R for "language and sexuality." This vague type of warning is not even given for most films, including *The Gingerbread Man*.

World's moral blind-spot about the evil methods of Hollywood is remarkable for two reasons: first, its mission statement, which declares the magazine's purpose:

> To help Christians apply the Bible to their understanding of and response to everyday current events. To achieve this by reporting the news on a weekly basis in an interesting, accurate, and arresting fashion. To accompany reporting with practical commentary on current events and issues from a perspective committed to the final authority of the Bible as the inerrant written Word of God. To assist in developing a Christian understanding of the world, rather than accepting existing secular ideologies.

Sadly, when it comes to entertainment, the Bible's authority and a "Christian understanding of the world" seem to become unimportant. Not only does *World* refuse to condemn indecency in any meaningful way, but also these morally objectionable elements are not even mentioned! Nothing could demonstrate more truly how accustomed the church has become to the things of the world. Our comfort with the world's immodest and impure ways is complete.

World's moral blind-spot is remarkable to me for a second reason. From my understanding, the views of publisher Joel Belz are in essential harmony with my own. When *World* magazine started, it filled a big need in my life. I got the "other" perspective on the news: the Christian viewpoint. Still in its infancy, *World* seemed a dream come true. I believed such a pioneering work deserved the full support of Christians everywhere. My one disappointment was the arts page, for the issues of message *and* methods were seldom addressed. Reviews had a Christian spin, but only in terms of the overall message. Little attention, if any, was given to the methods—the actual moral, visual content.

One review that really hit me hard was for the epic *Dances with Wolves*. Since this film had passed through the film lab in which I was working, I knew it contained nudity and a fairly explicit fornication scene. *World*'s review never mentioned these; it seemed to recommend the film without even a content warning. I wrote to a Mr. Lutz, the arts page editor, and received back this very gracious letter dated January 1991 from Joel Belz, then executive editor of *World*.

Dear Mr. Wilson,

Mr. Lutz passed on your letter of December 17. He and I have discussed it, and are in full agreement that we erred in publishing the review of *Dances with Wolves* as it stood.

Certainly you are correct we should have provided the warning which you suggest concerning the nude scenes and sexual explicit material.

Indeed, had we realized the film included this material, we almost certainly would not have published the review we did. Although we depended in this case on a reviewer whose judgment we trust very much, we think he should have told readers of this material. We take full responsibility, however, for the review, and do not want to appear to be "passing the buck."

We apologize for this offense, and hope you will pray that we do a better job along the way of trying to reflect biblical values. Obviously, to do so in the area of movie reviews is like walking through a minefield. We need God's special grace.

Of course, I was delighted with the response. I was touched by Mr. Belz's humility and openness to criticism. It said volumes about the man that he even took the time to write me. I wanted to thank him and wrote back directly:

Dear Mr Belz,

Thank you for your prompt response to my letter to Mr. Lutz regarding your review of the film *Dances with Wolves*. I was quite satisfied with your response and I appreciate you taking the time to discuss the matter with Mr. Lutz.

My purpose in writing was to make you aware of growing concerns about the content of entertainment with which Christians routinely involve themselves. There seems to be an absence of discussion regarding proper standards. I am a film buff, and formerly a film student, but when I became a Christian I realized that there are standards and it is at least worth discussing them and attempting to stimulate one another to holiness. My fear is that the leading lights in Christian discussions of the arts seem more interested in art than holiness. I would rather start with holiness and find where art fits in than start with whatever art exists and simply look for any point of compatibility with a Christian world view. A distinction must be made between pointing out the world's philosophy as expressed in its art, even obscene art, and recommending it as entertainment.

You are right when you say that the area of movie reviews is a minefield. I am sorry if I exploded under your feet. Still, your own analogy would call for extreme caution as one proceeds. Weigh carefully what your publication encourages believers to participate in, give money to, or enjoy. The idea that it is perfectly acceptable for believers to amuse themselves with actors simulating copulation is a rather new idea, you must admit. Two thousand years of church history is uniform in its condemnation of such amusements. If we are going to rewrite the book on this, we had better explain why in the light of Scripture and the overwhelming testimony of the teachers of the church. My own belief is that we must come to grips with the Scripture and a good place to start is Ephesians 5:1–14.

My prayers are with you. I hope *World* continues to become all it has the potential to become.

Sadly, I noticed little change in *World* beyond the short term, though I still found too much value in the magazine to cast it aside. But minefields are dangerous whenever they are transgressed. I stepped on another mine in April 1995 with

Pamela Johnson's review of the R- rated *Rob Roy*. She loved it, despite its blatant immodesty. The film had so much flagrant nudity that Christian writer Lael Arrington wryly refers to it as "Debbie Does Scotland"[5] . My biggest concern, as I have detailed in chapter 4, was Johnson's declaration that "the mark of a good film is not whether it details or tries to ignore the depravity of man, but within what context man's depravity is explored." That is, as long as the overall message is compatible with virtue, the actual content, the methods and means, are not fit for moral judgment. Now short one leg, I painfully decided to cancel my subscription to *World*, for it was now offering a philosophical justification for worldly amusements. I wrote them, a part of which follows:

> Question: what do you think Jesus would say on the set of *Rob Roy* when the director tells the actors to disrobe? My guess is He would not say: "It has a moral theme ladies, really." I doubt He would compliment the director for his "unblinking" portrayal of real life. The art reviewer's everything-I-see-and-do-is-OK-cause-I'm-a-critic attitude wears pretty thin in the light of God's holiness as expressed through His word.
>
> Rather than simply printing Pamela Johnson's opinions, you need to sit down with some biblical scholars and pastors and discuss the relevant scriptures related to the subject of immoral content *regardless of context*. Start with Christ, and let your public endorsement of films flow from Him on what is or is not a "high piece of artistry." The idea that skillfully wrought movie-making justifies robbing performers and the audience members of their

sense of shame and modesty needs to be repented of. No movie is worth the corrupting of one soul. Not one.

You can probably tell I was a little steamed. It's hard not to be indignant when purity is so rare and so many Christians are overwhelmed with sexual sin. I think they often don't know why immorality is such a problem, but when you know the images and ideas they constantly feed on, it is not hard to see. When Christian leaders, in print, on the web, or by example, deliberately overthrow purity, it is heartbreaking.

Needless to say, this time I received no response from *World*. By 1995, Marvin Olasky had replaced Joel Belz as editor, and Belz was listed as publisher. I have no idea if he saw my final letter. I got used to being without *World*, but then one day at the end of 1997, while perusing the journal of the American Family Association, I spied a commentary by Joel Belz. It was an excellent wake-up call about immoral images in films loved by Christians. He even singled out the sacrosanct *Braveheart*. This Joel Belz sounded a lot like the Joel Belz who wrote me in 1991. His commentary concluded:

> For Christians to think they can consume such a visual entertainment diet and not be affected is to think of ourselves much more highly than we ought to think. What makes it right to gaze with fascination at simulated "public displays of affection" when we wouldn't tolerate a glance at the real thing? It's a rationalization too many of us have passed on unthinkingly to our sons and daughters. It's also a rationalization it's time to reject.[6]

I was thrilled. Someone is finally saying what needs to be said, I thought. The commentary was reprinted from *World* magazine. Things had changed! I resubscribed to *World* right away. But alas, *World*'s arts-and-culture commentary had not changed; in fact, it had grown worse. It's labeling of *The Gingerbread Man* as "a good movie" and an "excellent morality tale" was an encouragement to readers to see the picture, despite its R-rated sexual content. The *Great Expectations* review was even worse, failing altogether to mention the offensive elements, which was remarkable since every secular review I read of *Great Expectations* carefully warned the reader about the film's moral content. The world was a better shepherd of the soul than *World* magazine!

I don't know what goes on at *World* magazine. My assumption is that Joel Belz, as publisher, gives his department heads a free hand. This must be the case, as it seems clear that their work contradicts his own views. This was demonstrated in *World*'s December 12, 1998, issue in which editor Olasky offered his own list of favorite films. At least three times he mentioned that his selection wouldn't sit well with some readers. Many of Olasky's favorite films contain explicit nudity, very foul language, and celebrate fornication. Olasky loves the word *compensation*. As long as a film has some idea or principle he agrees with, the evil elements are compensated for. Of course, he assures us, all the films he recommends are "wonderfully directed and acted." Once again, art needs no justification.

I have not written Joel Belz again. He has it right, but either he cannot or will not bring his contributors under the same moral principles he expressed so clearly as an editorialist. I will let my subscription run out again.

Others

World is hardly alone in this compromising philosophy. A number of Christian publications and Internet web sites have fallen into the same way of thinking. I do not believe they have deliberately set out to compromise standards. Somehow they have been lulled or overwhelmed into compromise. Why? I'm not sure. It is perhaps partly personal failure on the part of some. Having been seduced by Hollywood, like many others, they live by their feelings first. Part of the problem may be the reviewer's job itself. When 95 percent of Hollywood's product is evil, and your job is to comment on it, I suppose it gets tiresome to put it all in the same trash can. Many believers who love film cling to any sign of consistency with Christian belief, even if the "details of depravity" are in fact depraved.

It's nice to look for the positive, but it is wrong to succumb to the world's standards. Perhaps the greatest problem is the fatal spiritual disease of wanting to be seen as sophisticated. Who wants to be the fundamentalist reviewer, all hung up on a little nudity and sex? *World's* film reviews frequently carry a smug and sarcastic tone. The desire to be seen as intellectual and above such concerns as exposed flesh must be a great temptation. It should be resisted as such.

James admonishes us that Christians in positions of responsibility, whether in the pulpit, in the print media, or behind the camera, will be held to a higher standard (James 3:1). It is not a burden, but a glorious privilege to guide the flock to safer pastures. Compromise must end. God's people do not need permission from leaders of the evangelical community to see whatever strikes their fancy. They need guidance from the Word of God.

From the Swine's Point of View

The very idea of seeing a Hollywood feature made by an avowed evangelical was a cause of genuine excitement for me in the mid-1980s. Adding to the excitement was the film director's name: Schaeffer, the son of Francis Schaeffer, whose books had meant a lot to me in my early college days. Also, I had received a postcard in the mail, requesting my patronage for this new film. I didn't need to be asked twice. I called Scott, my lifelong friend and film-school buddy, and on the day *Wired to Kill* opened, we made our way down to one of the large theaters on Hollywood Boulevard to catch a matinee.

We were a little disappointed once inside. Only about six people were in the theater, and we wanted this film to succeed. Yet, as the reels of film unspooled, presenting the

vision of Franky Schaeffer to us, Scott and I were increasingly glad that only six people were sharing our experience.
We groaned, fidgeted, rolled our eyes, and yawned. *Wired to
Kill* proved to be one of the worst movies ever made. Up
until that time I thought Franky Scaeffer's book *Addicted to
Mediocrity* was a criticism of the evangelical subculture, not
a declaration of his personal goal. I left the theater very de-
pressed, wondering once again why in modern times all the
talent belonged to the world and none to the church.

It has been over a dozen years since I saw *Wired to Kill*,
but what I remember about it, besides its utter lack of energy
or wit or suspense, was the meanness that drove the story.
The film was about revenge, a theme Hollywood has masterfully handled in many great films, such as *Ben-Hur*, *The Searchers*, *The Bravados*, *Nevada Smith*, and many others. Those
films all come to the conclusion that revenge is ultimately
unsatisfying. They agree with Jesus that it is wrong. Schaeffer,
on the other hand, delighted in twisted and perverse means
of inflicting pain on the "bad guys." I wondered then, and
still wonder today, what drove Schaeffer's heart to express
his "art" in such terms.

I thought I might get some answers when Schaeffer wrote
his second book on the arts, *Sham Pearls for Real Swine*. I
didn't get my answers, but the same spirit which inspired
Wired to Kill animates every chapter of this book. Schaeffer,
using invective instead of argument, works hard to persuade
the reader that Christians who object to filthy language, naked bodies, sexual acts, and graphic violence in their entertainment are shallow, antirational, emotional, tasteless hypocrites and legalists. They are "real swine."

Because Schaeffer's book represents, in print, the dominant view of today's evangelical elite, it deserves attention. It is a difficult book to respond to, not because it is so compelling, but because its shotgun approach against all things disagreeable to Schaeffer makes a reasoned response challenging. In addition, the book contains a few frustrating contradictions. Schaeffer identifies himself as an artist throughout—a "Christian in the arts"—but then concludes, "I have no illusions that my work is art."[1] Nevertheless, he is deeply offended that Christians find his films so poor. He believes artists have every right to explore sexuality using nude models and actresses, yet he puts sexual fidelity first on a list of "the hardest challenges of the artistic life."[2] Schaeffer explains that he did not see Scorcese's *Last Temptation of Christ* because "as a believing Christian I am careful about what images I wish to absorb."[3] But any other believer who is careful about images in accordance with the Bible's own teaching on lust and modesty Schaeffer brands as a Pharisee and a hypocrite.[4]

Schaeffer's obsessive disdain for both Bible-believing Christians and popular culture wildly distorts his reading of history. To him, only modern fundamentalists are so boorish as to find something unsavory in good "real" sex acted out on the big screen (in context, of course).[5] Schaeffer sees the tide of church history completely on the side of his views. In a chapter on censorship, he even marshals the Puritans, claiming that the Puritans of the seventeenth century were "far more open-minded than their contemporary namesakes."[6] The fact is, these supremely literate and biblical people stood firmly against just the sort of things

Schaeffer is so fond of. The Puritans far exceeded the strict-
est fundamentalists of our day in absolute rejection of the
theatrical arts. As Bruce Daniels notes in his excellent book
Puritans at Play, "Elizabethan and early New England Puritans felt no ambivalence toward theater: it was evil, pure
and simple."[7] The Puritans would have had no film depart-
ments at their universities as do modern fundamentalist
schools, such as Bob Jones University.

Schaeffer makes a big mistake in his chapter on nudity in
art throughout church history. He assumes that representa-
tional art in painting or sculpture is equivalent morally to
photographic nudity in film or live nudity on stage. This is a
big jump deserving separate consideration (see the following
chapter). Even without issues of nudity and sexual acts, the
dominant position of the church on the theater is one of
condemnation in all eras, and from every Christian denomination. As pointed out in chapter three, I have found it extremely difficult to find any significant church figure writing
in favor of the theater—especially of secular theater—until
the era of modern evangelicalism, the era that Schaeffer so
thoroughly condemns.

I believe Schaeffer intends to criticize fundamentalism's
lack of sophistication in the arts, compared to earlier ages in
the church. In this he is probably right to an extent, but
even here he tends to forget that for a thousand years, the
church was the elite societal structure. It attracted the best
and the brightest talents because it was one of the few insti-
tutions that could support the arts at all. Modern, Bible-believing Christianity occupies no such place in our society for
a number of reasons. It could be argued that we have had

more important matters to attend to than building cathe-
drals or hiring someone to paint murals on ceilings. Schaeffer
forgets that most American Christians have not been raised
in Europe with personal exposure to the arts community. They
are just people, "not many wise, not many noble." In his hatred for modern, "plastic" fundamentalism, Schaeffer blinds
himself to the fact that, although the church supported the
arts much more in centuries past, there were still artistic standards that godly Christians held to. There was always a concern about the church becoming worldly, and there is abundant evidence that the wealthy, politically involved church,
which patronized the arts, became very worldly indeed.

Schaeffer perceives 1950s American culture as a kind of
phony world in which greatness ceased to exist. It was too
nice. (He doesn't consider that those men and women who
lived through the Depression and the Second World War
might have wanted it nice for a change.) Schaeffer attacks
Christian leaders who call for more wholesome entertainment—the dreaded "traditional values." He wrote:

> More often than not, what these offerings turn out to be
> is middle-class pablum that will offend no one, cause no
> one to think, mean nothing, and leave its audience as
> comfortable and mindless as before they were fleetingly
> entertained by it. In other words, the "traditional values"
> of the 1950s middle America, not the far more robust tra-
> ditions of Western culture. What most Christians seem
> to crave when they call for a Christian presence in the
> arts is a return to middle-American sentimentality, the
> kind of sentimentality that confuses virtue with niceness.[8]

This is, of course, untrue and unfair. People with standards of decency drawn from the Bible do enjoy good works of drama and films that make one think, that mean something, and that leave one feeling deepened by the experience of having been in the theater. The morality of the 1950s was the accepted morality of hundreds of years of Christian civilization. "Traditional values" or what might be called respect for common decency, were the values of Hollywood's Golden Era, the late 1930s through the 1940s. This is the time when censorship was at its peak in Hollywood. One could hardly describe *The Ox-Bow Incident*; *Good-bye, Mr. Chips*; *A Tale of Two Cities*; *Beau Gest*; *The Gunfighter*, or scores of other great films as "pablum."

Is their only crime that they knew how to handle grown-up themes tastefully? In an age when Batman beds his tipsy love-interest on their first date, some of us would prefer the Robin Hood of the 1930s, who defended and honored women, and even married his true love. We may even prefer the sophisticated adult comedy *The Philadelphia Story*, in which Jimmy Stewart does not take advantage of a tipsy Katharine Hepburn because "there are rules about such things."

And what of the 1950s in Hollywood? Is *On the Waterfront* pablum because the actors keep their clothes on and don't use filthy language? Does good taste mar the artistic worth of *Shane, Friendly Persuasion, The Red Badge of Courage*, or *To Kill a Mockingbird*? No. That is what Christians who honor the Bible long to see again. Old Hollywood proved that depicting truth is not dependent on exposing every piece of garbage that litters life. Truth can reveal, but also respect.

That is the secret the era of censorship taught us. That is the lesson Franky Schaeffer missed along the way.

Schaeffer's other mistake is equating Christianity with European civilization, as though anything done by a baptized European is "Christian" and an important part of the Christian teaching tradition. Thus Shakespeare becomes a "hero of the faith" in Schaeffer's mind, and as a hero of the faith, his bawdy humor becomes sanctified.[9] Shakespeare was a genius with the English language and with character development, and certainly, along with other playwrights of his day, he had an educated awareness of the Bible and of Christian morality. But it is equally certain that none of Shakespeare's many plays and sonnets reveal a passion for Jesus Christ or the gospel of grace. So, though western culture has been influenced by the church and the Bible, it has also absorbed many other influences contrary to Christianity.

Schaeffer likewise represents Rembrandt as a "hero of the faith." He shares how Christian it was for Rembrandt to paint a nude portrait of his wife waiting in bed for him. Somehow this painting is supposed to tell us that Christ is the Lord of all of life.[10] Knowing a little about Rembrandt's life, we might suspect he had a problem keeping his sexual life under Christ's lordship. Indeed, Rembrandt ignored requests to appear before a local church council to explain his living arrangements with his second mistress. He finally allowed her to stand before the church leaders alone, without his presence or support, and face the charges. She repented sufficiently, it seems, to allow Rembrandt's illegitimate child to be baptized. The painter himself could not be bothered with the church, nor with the middle-class morality Schaeffer finds so pathetic.

Christians are not obligated to see artist's wives in the altogether, in paint or on film. One might even blush, arriving at the artist's house one day and being shown his latest work. "This is my wife waiting in bed for me," he announces. As unforgivably middle-class as it might be, one might be tempted to respond, "How nice, but isn't that a matter between the two of you?"

Franky Schaeffer does not seem interested in the opinions of church leaders any more than Rembrandt was. Even though teaching pastors are Christ's gift to the church, according to Scripture, Schaeffer is more concerned with what artists in European countries have chosen to do rather than what the church has taught. He cites, for example, that nudity in art was common even in the Victorian era. But the greatest preachers of that era would sound positively "fundamentalist" if Schaeffer bothered to ascertain their positions on worldly amusements. Schaeffer continually pleads for freedom for the arts, freedom to expose and explore anything. Spurgeon, the great Victorian-era preacher, knew of such men in his day:

> I believe that one reason why the church of God at this present moment has so little influence over the world is because the world has so much influence over the church. Nowadays, we hear Nonconformists pleading that they may do this and do that—things which their Puritan forefathers would rather have died at the stake than have tolerated. They plead that they may live like worldlings. My sad answer to them, when they crave this liberty, is, "Do it if you dare. It may not cause you much hurt, for you are so bad already. Your cravings show how rotten

your hearts are. If you have a hungering after such dog's meat, go, dogs, and eat the garbage!"

Worldly amusements are fit food for mere pretenders and hypocrites. If you were God's children, you would loathe the very thought of the world's evil joys. Your question would not be, "How far may we be like the world?" but your one cry would be, "How far can we get away from the world? How much can we come out of it?" Your temptation would be rather to become more sternly severe, and ultra-Puritanical in your separation from sin, in such a time as this, than to ask, "How can I make myself like other men and act as they do?"[11]

Spurgeon was not a creation of 1950s American values. He was the greatest preacher of the Bible in his day. The fact is, Franky Schaeffer and Charles Haddon Spurgeon cannot both be right. One of them does not reflect the moral teaching of Christianity regarding sensual entertainment.

In the end, one suspects there may be more (or perhaps I should say less) to all this exposed flesh than artists like to believe. Francis Schaeffer, Franky's father, opened my eyes to the truth behind much of supposedly Christian art with nude figures. In *How Should We Then Live*, the elder Schaeffer discussed a portrait of the baby Jesus and the mother Mary by the French artist Fouquet. Mary has a breast fully exposed in the portrait, and Schaeffer tells us the picture is actually that of Agnes Sorel, the mistress of the king. Schaeffer wrote,

> the painting might be titled *The Red Virgin*, but the girl was the king's mistress; and when one looked at the

painting one could see what the king's mistress's breast looked like.[12]

The subject was biblical, but the reality was a kind of naughty joke.

One is reminded of the early, silent biblical epics of Cecil B. DeMille, in which all sorts of sensual and immodest displays are justified by a religious theme. Catholic authors Frank Getlein and Harold Gardiner, in their thoughtful *Movies, Morals, and Art* (1961) found the DeMille method to be old news.

> In French academic painting and sculpture of the nineteenth century may be seen the same combination of salacious effect with an atmosphere of either cultural uplift or religious edification: nude female victims of the slave trade, Christian martyrs from whom the lions have delicately torn the draperies before tearing the flesh, the full range of scenes from classical mythology *au naturel*, and all the virtues and vices symbolized by the same young lady with bared bosom. When photography itself became widely practiced, just over a hundred years ago, there appeared studio-posed scenes, in imitation of French paintings, in which large numbers of undressed girls represented the troubles of the Prodigal Son, or the Two Ways of Life, or anything else that might at once titillate the audience and allow it to believe it was being morally edified.
>
> It is a moot point whether outright pornography is worse in its effect than this blatant hypocrisy. [13]

The truth is, much of nudity in art, especially film, is tainted far more by prurient interest than a desire to reflect reality or beauty. Sex is good business, and even movie directors get a kick out of seeing actresses nude. That is a sad fact.

In the next chapter, I will discuss Schaeffer's views of entertainment in more detail. As a fundamentalist minister who is easily offended by immodest speech and dress, I suppose I should be offended by Schaeffer's accusation of pharisaical hypocrisy, but I'm not. As far as Schaeffer's view of prudish fundamentalism goes: better a pig in Franky Schaeffer's eyes than a reprobate in the eyes of the Lord.

Chapter Fifteen

Is the Bible Rated X?

Franky Schaeffer suggests that if the Bible were made into a movie, "it would be R-rated in some parts, X-rated in others." "The Bible," he tells us, "is not middle class. The Bible is not *nice*. The Bible's tone is closer to that of the late Lenny Bruce than to that of the hushed piety of some ministers."[1] I think it is fair to say that this claim is central to Schaeffer's argument that Christians need not limit what they see in entertainment and that artists have no moral obligation to limit themselves if their intent is truth, beauty, and all of that.

In *Sham Pearls for Real Swine*, Schaeffer suggests that the Bible itself is a "dangerous, uncivilized, abrasive, raw, complicated, aggressive, scandalous, and offensive book." This is because the Bible is untamed literature, a "rude challenge to false propriety."[2] Is it? Is the purpose of the Bible really to overthrow a culture built around sexual restraint and common decency? I hardly think so.

First of all, the Bible is not a movie. The medium of information matters a very great deal. The Bible contains no commands to act out every episode in explicit detail. The Bible was written in a time that predates film, among a people who did not express themselves theatrically. Is writing about an act of fornication or rape the same thing as painting a picture of it? Is it the same as asking a woman to act it out in all its details?

We read in Genesis 16:4 that Abraham "went in to Hagar, and she conceived." It is true that a sexual act has been described, but isn't this account as lacking in detail as possible to convey the information? We have no blow-by-blow description of Abraham's caresses or of Hagar's response. We know nothing of the act. Was it tender or formal? Brief or lengthy? Awkward or passionate? We don't know. That would not be the case had the act been filmed. Schaeffer knows this. Of course, the *story itself* could be filmed with no details included at all, and still present the information. That's how Old Hollywood would have done it. Abraham could have walked off toward a tent with Hagar and then we learn she is pregnant. The privacy of the characters or the performers need not be violated. We do not need to be keyhole peepers to learn what has occurred.

Yes, the Bible tells some sad stories of sin, but their sexual details are consistently avoided. "Reuben went and lay with Bilhah his father's concubine; and Israel heard of it" (Gen. 36:22). Raw? Uncivilized? Abrasive? The original incident is, but the recording of it is not. The rape of Dinah is recorded in these words: "Shechem the son of Hamor the Hivite, the prince of the land, saw her, he took her and lay with her by force" (Gen. 34:2). Had this been filmed with an actress allowing an actor to rip away her dress and force himself upon her, it would not be the same experience one would have reading these few words in the Bible. Schaeffer speaks as if they are equivalent descriptions, but they are not.

The only truly detailed sexual description in the Bible is the Song of Solomon. Schaeffer calls it "graphic sexuality." The word *graphic* suggests a picture, but Solomon does something in describing the joys of marital intimacy that is not graphic at all. He uses metaphor. Indeed, when I was a young man and tried to read the romantic Song of Solomon, I was rather disappointed. Without a reference point in experience, I really didn't know what Solomon was talking about. Solomon designed his poem for the initiated. This is a central point. Written accounts, especially such artfully and tastefully written accounts as we have in the Bible, are protective of innocence. It's just the sort of thing the "hushed piety" of some ministers would lead us to expect from God's Word. The truth is told, but the reader is not tempted with lustful images. God, James tells us in the Scripture, "does not tempt anyone." Innocence is protected while the truth is honored. Frank Gabelein says powerfully:

> "But what of the erotic passages in the Bible?" To that question, frequently raised by defenders of morally questionable literature, the answer can only be that the attempt to equate the restrained way in which Scripture

speaks of sex or the beautiful imagery of Solomon's Song
with a *Tropic of Cancer* or any other scatological novel is
sheer intellectual dishonesty convincing only to those who
are ignorant of Scripture.[3]

Schaeffer is a strong advocate of Neil Postman's writings
on television. He may have overlooked this very thoughtful
passage (partially quoted in chapter ten) from Postman's excellent book *The Disappearance of Childhood*:

> Like alphabetic writing and the printed book, televi-
> sion opens secrets, makes public what has previously been
> private. But unlike writing and printing, television has no
> way to close things down. The great paradox of literacy
> was that as it made secrets accessible, it simultaneously cre-
> ated an obstacle to their availability. One must qualify for
> the deeper mysteries of the printed page by submitting one-
> self to the rigors of a scholastic education. One must progress
> slowly, sequentially, even painfully, as the capacity for self-
> restraint and conceptual thinking is both enriched and
> expanded. I vividly remember being told as a thirteen-year-
> old of the existence of a book, Henry Miller's *Tropic of Can-
> cer*, that, I was assured, was required reading for all who
> wanted to know sexual secrets. But the problems that
> needed to be solved to have access to it were formidable.
> For one, it was hard to find. For another, it cost money. For
> still another, it had to be *read*. Much of it, therefore, was
> not understandable to me, and even the special passages to
> which my attention was drawn by a thoughtful previous
> reader who underlined them required acts of imagination
> that my experience could not always generate.

Television, by contrast, is an open-admission technology to which there are no physical, economic, cognitive, or imaginative restraints. The six-year-old and the sixty-year-old are equally qualified to experience what television has to offer. Television, in this sense, is the consummate egalitarian medium of communication, surpassing oral language itself. For in speaking, we may always whisper so that the children will not hear. Or we may use words they may not understand. But television cannot whisper, and its pictures are both concrete and self-explanatory. The children see everything it shows.[4]

It seems clear that thoughtful people, even non-Christians like Postman, find the concept of innocence something to be treasured rather than visually assaulted.

Although Schaeffer suggests a nearly limitless exposure to sexual images, as long as they are presented in an artistically valid context, one suspects that a biblically informed moral conscience still has some sway on his thinking. His own disastrous film, *Wired to Kill*, carefully avoided exposing the flesh of its young heroine, even when the villain had her hanging from the ceiling and vulnerable to any type of assault. Few R-rated, schlock movies like *Wired to Kill* would have avoided such an excellent opportunity to expose some skin. Schaeffer is to be commended.

Also, in Schaeffer's chapter "Naked Again," he defends nudity in art by emphasizing painting and sculpture instead of his mainstay: the cinema. Again he tries to emphasize the fact that the Bible records that people have been naked. He even mentions Noah naked in his tent, being gazed upon by his youngest son; but he seems to have missed altogether the curse that resulted from "looking and telling." Nor does Schaeffer mention the extreme care taken by Shem and Japheth not to look upon their father. Perhaps these sons were already showing behavior that anticipated the plastic, middle-class morality of the pietistic culture of legalistic fundamentalists. Or perhaps the attitude of any righteous person in any generation is to seek to cover another's shame, not photograph it.

Schaeffer appeals to church history for his primary defense of nudity in art. He takes a very negative view of Christians who approach moral problems "armed with our own reading of Scripture and our puny consciences."[5] He seems to foreshadow, here, his own later abandonment of the Protestant faith.

Still, an appeal to church history is not without merit. And it is certainly true that some church figures over the years found nudity in painting and sculpture an acceptable way to express certain ideas. Schaeffer lists a few of these ideas in his book. But since the subject here is really film and drama, we need to ask whether the nude figure in a painting is the same as undressed actors on the stage or in a film.

It seems to me the two experiences of the nude are quite different. To the viewer, photographic reality is reality. The person on display is a real person, not a representation of a person. The shamelessness of such a display of the body is evident. A painted nude may not be real at all. There may be a model, but there may not be as well. The painted nude may well be a work of the imagination. The great artist Raphael wrote, "To paint beauty I need to see many beauties, but since there is a dearth of beautiful women, I use a certain idea which comes into my mind." I'm not sure Raphael's mental activity benefited his soul, but it did separate his artwork from real women.

It needs to be said, as well, on the subject of the painted nude, that the common idea that artists are so into their work that they don't see their models in a sexual way is wishful thinking. The lives of artists do not show an unusual level of purity for having seen so many people undressed. Quite the opposite seems to be the norm. A friend of mine who attended Cal Arts, a prestigious arts college in southern California, run by the Disney company, told me that large on-campus parties sponsored by the school frequently become orgies of the sort one would expect to see in ancient Rome. Students openly have sex on stairwells and in public places with the staff having full knowledge of these affairs. Could it be that their minds are overloaded on things they shouldn't be seeing? It is a fair question.

There is an aesthetic argument against nudity in film that does not apply to painting in the same way. We have said that a naked person on film is really a naked *person*, not an abstraction. When film is at its best, the viewer forgets that he is watching a movie. He is so completely *held* by the film that he becomes a part of it. Anything that reminds him that he is watching a movie is considered an artistic failure. Things like out of place music, overly acrobatic camerawork, or an airplane in the sky in a western, can push the viewer out of the world into which he has been invited. Nudity, without question, has the same effect on many people. In a delightful editorial piece written in 1986, political columnist Joseph

Sobran showed real insight when he complained about nudity in film. He points out:

> Nudity in movies, far from being "necessary to the development of the story," is nearly always a distraction from the story, unless perhaps the story centers around a nudist colony. The moment a character disrobes, you become aware of him or her (usually her, of course) less as a character than as an actual human being.

Sobran cites the example of an Ann-Margaret strip scene in a film:

> I wasn't thinking about the character or plot anymore; only about the actress, her probable feelings, her husband, the cameraman, that sort of thing. The aesthetic dimension was disrupted. Reality had intruded on realism.

He finds the same problem with male nudity:

> When I see Jeremy Irons backside, say, in *Brideshead Revisited*, I cease thinking of the character he is playing and start musing about how a man would feel exposing his rump to the millions.[6]

It's true. Nudity takes us out of the cinematic experience and deposits us back in the real world—a shameful moment in the real world.

Consider, for example, the wedding-night scenes in two medieval epics: *El Cid* (1961) and *Braveheart* (1995). In *Braveheart*, the character Wallace marries his sweetheart secretly so that she will not be snatched away by the English baron, who would claim a (completely nonhistorical) right to lie with the brides of his underlings on their wedding night. They marry secretly because Wallace will not share her. Mel Gibson, who played Wallace and who directed the film, decided to share the wedding night with millions of moviegoers. He placed the camera and arranged the movement to highlight his leading lady's bare breasts. The scene is staged awkwardly at best and hardly natural.

In *El Cid*, we are not allowed into the private, intimate life of the newly married couple. We witness them as they are waking the next morning, now modestly attired. They are playful, happy, full of pleasant memories. It looks a lot like love. It is one of the finest snapshots of married love in the movies, yet we see nothing private or shameful. We are not voyeurs peeping under the curtains. We are an audience enjoying a worthy representation of marriage. The nudity in *Braveheart* actually detracts from the very thing it is supposed to represent. This leads me to believe it is placed there for other reasons.

Sometimes Hollywood's need to show a bit of flesh results in amusing assaults on the story line. A classic case is Kevin Costner's tedious version of an old legend: *Robin Hood, Prince of Thieves*. In the film, Maid Marion finds Robin quite boorish and unattractive until she spies him bathing in a stream. Critics scoffed at the notion that her feelings would change just because she saw his naked behind. The filmmakers had to explain that she softens toward Robin because she sees the marks of a brutal whipping on his back. Ironically, the moviemakers were so intent on including Costner's rear end that the audience can barely see, much less notice, the stripes on his back. So much for high art!

Again, in Schaeffer's chapter on nudity, he does not mention film or the stage. Yet later he implies that the arguments about painting apply to film. Schaeffer lists a number of his favorite films. It is difficult to imagine any of the church figures of the Renaissance (or artists for that matter) celebrating the kind of sexual content in the films Schaeffer finds so appealing, such as *Fatal Attraction, The Terminator, Blade Runner,* or *All That Jazz.* Schaeffer claims *Fatal Attraction,* a ludicrous film about a married man being stalked by a "one-night stand" with a butcher knife, is "a profamily movie if there ever was one."[7] For Schaeffer, the presence of a wife at home makes any silly Hollywood gorefest a profamily movie. This is typical of the moral error condemned by earlier writers on film and morality but accepted today—anything goes if you can toss a "redeeming" feature into the story somewhere. It's an old trick, and modern evangelical artists seem to have fallen for it in a big way.

Schaeffer claims *The Terminator* is "directly prolife in its implications." One wonders if most dating couples who saw this movie were moved to a prolife position, or if a more likely result was an excited libido from watching the two stars naked and copulating on a large screen. One can only speculate if their car ride home afterward was moved in the direction of a moral, philosophical discussion or an out-of-the-way parking spot.

Blade Runner is a classic example of nudity added solely for the purpose of titillation. It is a case study of nobody saying anything important while breasts are displayed. The important dialogue happens while careful and discreet camera angles are used. This is typical in films that are likely to be edited for network television, revealing the phony "necessity" of such content in the first place.

All That Jazz does describe the decline of a degenerate theater man. Sadly, many of the actresses are used shamefully, in completely unnecessary ways, for the purpose of sexually charging the audience. The film abounds with prurient nudity. This film, though of high quality production values, fits by any society's standards, the definition of *pornographic*. As in the painting of *The Red Virgin* in which people saw the breast of the king's mistress, *All That Jazz* disrobes the beautiful dancer Ann Reinking, among others. The question is: should Christian men choose to see this? Or should they, out of respect for Miss Reinking, choose not to?

Personally, I could live a full life having never seen one of these films. I don't believe any human life is diminished by missing them. Every positive virtue that might be shown by any one of them has been expressed better elsewhere with far less prurient elements. If Hollywood wants to tell these stories to decent people, let them be fashioned for decent people. This used to be a thoroughly understood concept, even by non-Christians. It is a sad day when Christian artists accuse God's people of being in the wrong for holding to a basic standard of common decency.

If only Christian artists, such as Schaeffer, had the sensibilities of truly great talents like Hermes Pan, the brilliant choreographer for Fred Astaire and for many of the best musicals ever made. He related in an interview that he and Mr. Astaire could have found their way around the censors under the old studio system, but he says, they never wanted to. Neither of these men ever wanted to offend someone who came to see their work. It would have hurt them to offend. Is Astaire diminished as an artist because he cared about the moral sensibilities of the audience? I think not. Indeed, who has done as much to elevate the dancer's art on film since his day has passed?

I do not believe I am on the fringe for suggesting that nudity undermines the moral order. This idea comes straight from the mind of those who want to see the moral order undermined. Amos Vogel, the founder-director of the New York Film Festival and the Lincoln Center Film Department, wrote a book called *Film as a Subversive Art*. He deals a lot with how film has been a major force for undermining religion and patriotism. He describes the benefits of showing things on the screen once deemed inappropriate.

> The attack on the visual taboo and its elimination by open, unhindered display is profoundly subversive, for it strikes at prevailing morality and religion and thereby at law and order itself. It calls into question the concept of eternal values and rudely uncovers their historicity. It proclaims the validity of sensuality and lust as legitimate human prerogatives. It reveals that what the state authority proclaims as harmful may in fact be beneficial. It brings birth and death, our first and last mysteries, into the arena of human discourse and eases their acceptance. It fosters rational attitudes which fundamentally conflict with atavistic superstitions. It demystifies life, organs, and excretions. It does not tolerate man as a sinner, but accepts him and his acts in their entirety.[8]

If Vogel is right, Schaeffer and those who think like him are a part of this subversion process. I would never believe they are intentionally part of it, but their wrong notions of morality, in contrast with the plain teaching of the Bible, have led countless Christians into the camp that seeks to strike at eternal values. The world knows what it is doing to us. Do we?

Schaeffer has created a false choice between "sham pearls" (his term for second-rate Christian art) and art that is tainted by worldly sensuality and vulgarity. If these were the only choices, then the church would have to choose second-rate Christian art or forsake the arts altogether. Perhaps a third way is better still, a way forged clearly in Hollywood's Golden Age. Quality art, that does not seek to violate morally the performers or the audience, can be created. It has been done. Although the nude is common in painting, it is in fact, less common than one might think compared to all the wonderful painting that has been done over the centuries. And on film, Hollywood has proven that great art—the highest cinematic artistry—needs neither naked flesh nor coarse language to succeed brilliantly. I believe we should walk down this third way for a richer life and a better society.

Taking
a Stand

It has been a long wait for those of you who say, "Don't give me a lot of theory, just tell me what I should do." You want practical advice. Here it is at last. I suppose I've taught the apostle Paul's letters so often that now that I am following his style: first the teaching, then the application. Of course, like Paul, I have not been able to resist addressing some application and challenges along the way, but in this final chapter, I want to move from principle to practice. I wrote this book to change behavior as well as thinking. If what you choose to *do* does not conform with God's word, then I have failed.

I want to start with some general advice to all of God's people living in the Age of Entertainment. The advice that follows is based on the moral understanding I have presented in this book. Then will follow specific advice according to our differing conditions in life.

Advice for Every Christian

First of all, recognize that the movies are a leading expression of the moral failure of our culture. The movies, as a rule, are not neutral. They delight in evil. There are exceptions, but the exceptions are rare. Accordingly, our attendance at the movies should be rare too. Theatergoing should not be something we do instead of playing miniature golf. Unlike putting, movies must be approached with extreme caution, as though one were treading into the domain of a deceitful and powerful enemy, for that is the truth of it. Critical faculties must be on full alert. Christians must never randomly patronize the theater. A film's popularity should make no difference. You should be willing to remain ignorant of the "movie event of the year" if it violates God's standard. Believe me, He is not impressed by the Academy Awards.

Ultimately, the whole issue comes down to your perspective, your attitude toward evil. How do you see evil? Does your heart see uncleanness and impurity as God does? Does your heart ache, along with His, over sin and immorality? The Scripture says simply, "Abhor what is evil; cling to what is good" (Rom. 12:9). To abhor something is to want nothing to do with it. Is that where your heart is? Or have the pleasures of the world, as set forth in the movies, shaped your heart to *tolerate* what is evil, instead of abhorring it? If so, repentance may be in order before you proceed.

You must decide to make entertainment standards as firm and true as those regarding other areas of sin and compromise. Bring your choices of amusement directly under the lordship of Christ. He must be the Lord of laughter and tears, thrills and adventures. Entering a theater or turning on a television is done in His presence. Because Jesus' lordship must be acknowledged at all times, here are some practical steps that will help you submit this area of your life to Him.

PRAY ABOUT EACH ENTERTAINMENT CHOICE

Believers are very careful to pray over their food—something which bears only upon the body. Theatrical amusements are food for the soul. How many believers do you know who pray over what they watch? I suggest you never go to a movie or rent a video without asking the Lord Jesus to help you choose well and worthily. Ask Him to bless your choice. Submit your choice to Him. Tell Him that you desire to honor Him by patronizing only that which is wholesome and consistent with the moral principles of His Word. Tell Him that if you choose poorly, you will walk out or turn it off.

If Christians would do this one thing, the whole entertainment issue would be over. In fact, I believe that if every Christian did this, Hollywood would be in dire financial straits. They would be compelled to turn out more films that Christians could support without compromise. Our numbers are that significant. Prayer could usher in a new Golden Age of cinema.

HAVE ADVANCED CONTENT INFORMATION

Never go to a movie without clear knowledge of its content. Many PG movies are unworthy of Christian patronage. As I said in chapter 12, do not rely on the rating system. Fortunately, there are several ways to gain content information. The best way is on the Internet. Probably the best Internet site for film content is "Screen It!" which can be found at: www.screenit.com

Screen it! offers very detailed reviews of content elements from a secular perspective. The reviews themselves do not follow biblical morals, but the extensive descriptions of any possible objectionable content are excellent. The site deals with immodesty (even telling you when there is "cleavage"), language (in great detail), violence, bad attitudes, scary scenes, alcohol and drug use, and much more. The only weak point at this site is the failure to address the moral ideas of some situations. For example, *Screen it!* considers Zorro's slicing away a woman's clothes until she is topless "mild nudity" because her hair is over her breasts. But the *idea* of the hero playfully slicing off a woman's clothing is meant to be titillating and is plainly detrimental to good morals. It's an image no Christian boy should have in his mind to take with him to the playground. Every time he picks up a toy sword, that image will return because Zorro's skill was blended with a direct appeal to his sexual nature. Few critics consider the pure heart.

"Critics, Inc." was the first online movie guide. Until late in 1998, this service was featured on America Online, but was removed rather abruptly, possibly because of vicious letters from fans of *Titanic*, which was panned by "Critics, Inc." reviewer Brandon Judell. "Critics, Inc." has, as part of their service, a feature called "Kids-in-Mind," which offers brief, but fairly helpful, content reviews. "Kids-in-Mind" also uses a one-through-ten scale for sex/nudity, violence, and language. Though bounced from AOL, "Kids-in-Mind" can be found on the Internet at www.kids-in-mind.com.

There are several Christian Internet sites devoted to informing believers about content in current films. Unfortunately, I have found only one that comes close to upholding the standards outlined in this book. The "Childcare Action Project" takes a serious and biblical view of evil in the movies. The Internet address is www.capalert.com.

"Childcare Action Project" has two drawbacks. The rating system of using thermometers and the MPAA rating system on a variety of categories, can get a little confusing. But as you spend time with the system, it makes more sense. The reviews themselves offer direct advice as though standards really mattered. Most Christian web sites treat immorality as an opinion, basing everything on what might offend individual tastes, as though God has no objective standard. "Childcare Action Project" avoids that trap. Its other drawback is a lack of timely information. The site covers only a few of the current releases, and it often picks up films after they've been out a few weeks, which means many people have already seen them. I believe an effort is being made to improve this. "Childcare Action Project" is to be commended for standing firm on the Bible and the lordship of Jesus Christ.

Other Christian web sites suffer from one fatal problem: a lack of definite standards. The mood and opinion of the reviewers, rather than the Word of God, determine recommendations. They operate as if moral principles in entertainment are all gray. The result is that these web sites routinely endorse movies that are truly worldly, even shamefully evil. They cannot find the strength to say that popular films are unworthy of Christian patronage. Their standards shift with the culture. What was "evil" a few years ago is a "caution" today.

I believe there is a problem inherent in being a Christian film reviewer. The barrage of immoral amusements takes a toll on the reviewer himself. After seeing so much that a Christian should not see—so much skin, so much sexual play and innuendo, hearing so many bad words—after a time it no longer shocks. Sheer exposure makes very wicked images and ideas seem routine. Reviewers can rarely be trusted to maintain a standard, especially if their standards were subjective from the beginning. Calling film after film "evil" gets pretty boring as well. Reviewers start to look for any positive element that justifies Christian patronage. Pretty soon, they are recommending trash. Some Christian web sites are positively corrupting—and proud of it.

For those without computers, try major newspapers. *The Los Angeles Times* runs their "Weekend Calendar" section on Thursdays and offers a "Family Filmgoer" feature that is much like "Kids-In-Mind." Unaware parents would have known about *Titanic's* nudity had they consulted this source.

Even if you have just a telephone, you can call a "Movie Review Line" sponsored by the Catholic Church. They have their own rating system, which is far superior to that of the MPAA. It is a toll-free call at 1-800-311-4222. Remember, however, that their standards are still age-based. Many films the Bible would forbid to all Christians, this service recommends for adults. Still, they are pretty tough. *Titanic* got an A-III—"adults only"—rating, and the latest PG-13 James Bond movie received an O for morally offensive—that is, to be shunned by all decent people. There is no excuse for going to the movies uninformed.

TAKE JESUS WITH YOU

The current fad of wearing WWJD insignia doesn't seem to translate into direct action for very many people. But it is the right question: What *would* Jesus do? What would be His attitude toward shameful entertainment? Would He feel left out if He missed the latest blockbuster movie? Would He be content to hear His Father's name used again and again as a curse? Would He laugh at toilet humor, cheer revenge, gaze at a young woman who was shamefully exposed? To ask such questions is to answer them. All that's left to ponder are the words of Jesus Himself, "And why do you call Me, 'Lord, Lord,' and do not do what I say?"

REMEMBER WHOSE MONEY YOU'LL BE SPENDING

Your money is God's money. You are a steward of His gifts. Do not use His gifts to support evil. The purchase of a ticket is a vote for a movie's content. It is the only opinion poll Hollywood cares about. Will you buy a ticket? Will you rent a video? If you do, you declare "I approve." That is all they know.

AVOID THE TV MISTAKE

Unfortunately, many Christians who wouldn't frequent the movies fail to carefully monitor their televisions. Hollywood television, as a rule, is no better than Hollywood movies. And most Hollywood movies have the largest audience when they show on television. At one time, Hollywood movies were "edited for television." Language was toned down, skin scenes snipped out, etc. This is less and less the case, and the TV industry now produces shows and movies with nudity and foul language. This is no longer true only of special, pay cable channels. Networks and basic cable channels have all gone in this direction. I can write with confidence that, by the time this book moves from writing to publication, more objectionable material will be found on regular television than was there the year before. It never gets better, only worse. But like the proverbial frog in the kettle, Christians acclimate to the changing TV climate until they are well-cooked and their children robbed of innocence.

Turner Network Television (TNT), for example, which boasts being the best movie studio on television, nearly always includes scenes of nudity in their films, be it *The Rough Riders* or a film about Peary and Henson reaching the North Pole. Skin scenes have become so common on TNT that many observers believe that it has become a network requirement. Of course, TNT, like Hollywood before it, built its reputation with very fine and morally uplifting presentations, such as Turner's excellent *Gettysburg*. Unfortunately, it has been on a downhill slide ever since. Even TNT's history-based films have become outrageously inaccurate, always choosing politically correct revisionism over truth.

Regular channels are still mostly about teasing and tempting. It is the pay cable channels that are the major source of pornographic addiction in America today. Sadly, channels such as HBO are offered free to some cable subscribers. Do not take it. You may as well lay copies of *Playboy* on your coffee table and tell your children not to look at it, if you tolerate HBO in your home. HBO's programming is loaded with nudity, sex, and the worst language imaginable. Do you know what the highest-rated show on HBO is? No, it's not those Emmy-winning movies. It is their explicit sex "documentaries" called *Real Sex*. It is pure porn, and it serves as a transition point on one channel from PG-13 and R-rated filth, to full pornography. Do not allow this channel in your home. If you have cable TV, you can block any channel from coming into your home. Call your cable company. Do not allow HBO, Showtime, The Movie Channel, etc. access to your family. Refuse to support these companies financially.

One firm principle that should be maintained without compromise regarding the television and VCR. Never have a television in the children's bedroom. Do not put a TV any place where it can be seen without direct oversight. There is way too much trash on virtually all channels now to allow unmonitored access to your child's heart. Easy access by children to a leading cause of moral depravity is simply foolish. Children who have hours alone at home (a sad reality in too many families) should not have TV as a companion. Television should be a minor player in the home, and it should be a family event when it is on.

In our home, we block many channels. We don't even get the major networks anymore. Television really is a vast wasteland. Don't be compromised by it. The danger is in its familiarity and easy access. Television time should be rare. As with the movies, it should be selectively and prayerfully viewed.

Advice for Parents

The most important thing a parent can do for a child is lead him or her to personal faith in Jesus Christ. This is the first duty of Christian parenting. The second duty, which follows closely on the heals of the first, is to protect the innocence of the child. Solomon returned again and again to the theme of sexual restraint in advising his son. The key to that restraint is a *heart* that is pure. "Do not desire her beauty in

your heart," he said of the evil woman (Prov. 6:25). The father was teaching the son about his thought life.

The problem of moral failure among Christian youth is a
tragedy of massive proportions. A large majority of churched
youth have lost their virginity before they've graduated from
high school, many more in their college years. I believe this
has slowly come to be expected in many churches and no longer
is considered a battle worth fighting. Or where it is fought, all
the energy is put into maintaining physical purity. That is not
God's standard. He desires mental purity, heart purity, from
His children. He knows how profoundly the mind and actions
are linked. We have failed to morally educate the minds of a
whole generation, but God's standard has not changed:

> For this is the will of God, your sanctification; that is,
> that you abstain from sexual immorality; that each of you
> know how to possess his own vessel in sanctification and
> honor, not in lustful passion like the Gentiles who do not
> know God . . . (1 Thess. 4:3–5)

Self-control over the body requires knowing *how* to avoid
lustful passions, the very subject dominating the entertainment industry. For some reason, when it comes to Hollywood,
we willingly send our children into situations where lustful
passions are set on fire. And we do it simply to grab a few
hours of meaningless pleasure for ourselves. You must teach
your child, and perhaps yourself, the *how* of moral purity,
which is guarding the heart and mind.

I also believe that the issue is more than just the tragic
fall of so many into sexual immorality. Modern churchgoing
young people are often possessed of a worldly frame of mind.

They have a jaded quality, a disturbing lack of innocence. The world holds little wonder for them, little joy. Happiness is increasingly associated with cheap thrills, rather than with the simple pleasures of living. It is hard for them to have genuine wholesome pleasures when their senses are pounded by Hollywood and when everything is tainted with sleaze.

Hollywood has so infused comedy and humor with the crude and the sexual, that naughtiness has become a part of our children's mental makeup. Humor with a measure of evil in it, twists the nature of a child. By combining laughter with sleaze, Hollywood robs children of innocent joy. Clean pleasures seem to lack something, because the heart has been trained to delight in evil. It used to be funny to see a dog bite a man on the leg. Then all bites had to be on the rear end. Now, in all films for all ages, dog bites and physical blows are always aimed at the genitalia. Because the humor involves the private parts, it comes with a sense of the naughty, the shameful. The child's heart is being prepared for coarser, more indecent fare. Pleasure is being systematically connected to that which is shameful and private.

Put yourself in the shoes of the modern child or teen who frequents the movies and watches television. They almost never go to the movies and see virtue in the area of sexuality. Virtually all of the movie heroes are fornicators. None of the men respect the virtue of women. None of the women are modest in speech, dress, or manner. Female role-models are extremely rare—almost nonexistent. One could argue the point that one movie won't influence a person. But the real issue is not the effect of one movie; it is the cumulative effect of movie after movie after movie. It is madness to believe this has no shaping influence on the soul of a child. Your concern as a parent should be the same as Jesus' concern for His church:

> that He might sanctify her, having cleansed her by the washing of water with the word, that He might present to Himself the church in all her glory, having no spot or wrinkle or any such thing; but that she should be holy and blameless. (Eph. 5:26–27)

Dads and Moms, do not compromise your child's innocence for entertainment's sake. Treasure the purity of your child's mind. Never expose your sons to lustful images or your daughters to romanticized fornication. Do not let them be corrupted by lewd jokes. Love them enough to say no. Your home is to be a sanctuary from the wickedness of the world. Your choices are the most influential moral factor in your children's lives.

I can tell you, from our own family's experience, that working with your children in this area can be most rewarding. It can succeed. We have cultivated our children's entertainment tastes by exposing them only to high-quality, decent entertainment. This means about a 90 percent reliance on the classics. My eldest daughter (thirteen now) does not know who Jim Carrey is. She has never seen an Eddie Murphy movie. She isn't gaga over Leonardo DiCaprio. She's never seen him. Her favorite comedian is Red Skelton, her favorite films: *Whistling in the Dark* and *A Southern Yankee*. She likes Judy Garland (*Meet Me in St. Louis*, *The Wizard of Oz*), and Judy with Mickey Rooney (*Strike Up the Band*, *Babes in Arms*, the Andy Hardy films). She likes *National Velvet*, *Bringing Up Baby*, and she does a pretty fair impression of James

Cagney in *White Heat*, her favorite cops-and-robbers movie. She enjoyed *Gone with the Wind* in the movie theater. We have not denied her music and laughter, drama and pathos. But we have guided her choices. You don't have to persuade a child to like great movies. They sell themselves. You must merely limit the influence of sleaze, so that is not connected in their minds with a "good film," and then give them access to greatness. It is nearly impossible for a little girl whose innocence has been guarded, not to enjoy *National Velvet*. Only a jaded child would find it lacking. There are many, many great films from Old Hollywood, and perhaps one or two a year from our own time that are pure and true and excellent.

We do not tempt our daughter away from the classics by watching Hollywood promotional shows on television, such as *Entertainment Tonight* or *Access Hollywood*. We even avoid the entertainment feature sections of news programs, which are little more than sales pitches for Hollywood's evil products. We don't buy magazines, such as *People*, that talk up Hollywood or celebrities. We don't idolize movie stars or care about their opinions. They are unimportant in our home. Most of the actors we enjoy have passed away now, anyway.

It is our hope that when our children are grown, they will associate decency with quality and continue to love and cherish the wholesome entertainment they now experience with such pleasure. We believe they will. We have seen them censor themselves on many occasions already; they phone us from a friend's home if a movie is to be shown, to ask if it will be alright. We have never had a battle over a worldly amusement. They seem to have truly adopted our standards for themselves, because they know they are God's standards, and we live by them too.

I must confess that we have several advantages in our home. As home-schoolers, we don't have the constant peer pressure to see the latest "fad" PG-13 movie. We have seen many parents cave in to their children's desires to see worldly movies. This is a terrible parenting failure. The enticement to pursue the world must be firmly resisted with patient and loving instruction. Children can understand biblical rules and what is or is not allowed in "our family." Also, as mentioned above, we don't give mixed signals to our children. Parents should live the biblical standard, not the age standard. Parents who see worldly movies because they are for "adults" send the wrong message to their children. Their actions declare that enjoying shameless behavior is something to be sought, like getting the rights to drive a car. But purity of mind and heart is not age-related in Scripture. How dare we exempt ourselves from biblical standards?

We also have had the advantage of raising our children this way from the beginning. I have noticed real challenges for parents who have become Christians when their children are already in their teens. It is not easy to adopt high standards after years of indulging in worldly amusements. You will have to be very open and honest about honoring the Lord in this area. Tell your children that you are learning and growing, that you were wrong in the past. They will respect your honesty about this (but some will not accept these standards for themselves). It is hard to return to innocence, impossible to do so without the new birth.

For some children who have been immersed in the world, it may take long years of sad experience to finally reject the world. It is a battle, but it must be waged. Set the example.

Learn to communicate the value of a pure mind and heart. Start to bring home some of the great classics—even modern kids enjoy them if given half a chance. But still, you must change what is allowed in *your* home. Don't compromise on decency. Do be patient and full of love. And offer meaningful alternatives. When a teen who has seen many PG-13 and R-rated movies is suddenly asked to give it all up, he or she will likely complain: "Oh, yeah, my mom and dad have gone nuts. They want us to turn into monks! They won't even let me watch *Batman!*" Respond with sincerity and humor. Be big-hearted, not rigid and narrow. But don't compromise.

Advice to Men

In the earliest pages of this book, I cited as an example of moral compromise a Christian congressman who took his Bible-study group to a sexually explicit, R-rated movie. My intent was to highlight the contrast between his stated goal (helping men be more faithful to their wives through fellowship) and his methodology (exposing them to sexual images). Of course, it was not his intent to cause his friends to stumble. What leaps out of the story is his failure to connect impure amusements to impure lifestyles. To him, R-rated fare was a means of fellowship, a way to relax. It never seemed to have entered his mind that this would be an offense to God, or that feeding on garbage is an unfit way to strengthen purity. This tells us how completely Hollywood has conquered Christian virtue. The entertainment world is so pervasive, most of us don't give it a second thought. We don't seek the Lord while we are perusing the paper for something to do. We don't pray. We don't ask God to honor himself in our choices. That is why we compromise.

Brothers, maintaining moral standards is up to us. In many—though by no means in *all*—homes, it is the men who lead the family to drink at the well of worldly entertainment. It's time to own up to our biblical responsibilities. The Bible's standard has not changed. Personal purity, even in our thoughts, is still what God wants. It is your job to teach your sons respect for women. Part of this is teaching him that women are not to be degraded for the sake of an hour's amusement. Show him that on a scale of choices, decency and respect are more important than fun. You can find fun in a thousand other ways. Your son must see you as a model of a man who, because of the covenant with his eyes, will not "gaze at a maiden." You must be the one to demonstrate wise entertainment choices and a heart that treasures purity.

See if you understand what drives the following conversation between a fifteen-year-old boy and his dad.

Boy: Dad, I want to meet my friends at the mall for a movie. Can I go?

Dad: What are you going to see?

Boy: Well, the guys really want to see *Meteor Wars*. It's a science-fiction movie.

Dad: I don't think so, Son.

Boy: But why? It's only PG-13.

Dad: I looked that movie up on the Internet. There's a lot of bad language and some sort of scene in a strip club.

Boy: But Dad, they couldn't show *that* much!

Dad: Son, I don't ever want you in a place like that. I would never take you into one, and I would never go

in one myself. I'm certainly not going to let your mind
enter one through a movie. I could never live with
myself if I put such a stumbling block in front of you.

Boy: But, Dad, don't you trust me?

Dad: No. I don't even trust me. God gave us this standard. Let's protect ourselves the way He said. I'd be a
fool to challenge His wisdom. There's more to it than
just a glimpse of flesh, though that's bad enough. I
don't ever want you to think about women the way
men do in places like that.

Boy: I don't want to.

Dad: But those ideas come from the images and ideas that
fill your heart. You can't filter out what you see, Son.
Once you've seen it, it's there. You know, the Bible
says to love young women like sisters, in all purity.
You wouldn't want your sister in a scene like that,
would you?

Boy: No way.

Dad: Me either. And those actresses are somebody's sisters and daughters. I'm sure there's some exciting
things in that movie, but we don't want to do anything that would displease Jesus, would we?

Boy: No, Dad. But the guys—

Dad: Might think you're not cool. I never believed much
in cool. There's a secret about that.

You will seem uncool when you act embarrassed
about your beliefs. But if you are courageous in standing up for what's right, you might get a little ribbing,
but I guarantee you, they will respect you. Now, let's
find something else to do, OK?

This Dad is leading his son in the path of righteousness. Lead your families, men. That is done by living a biblical standard and teaching it. As much good as organizations such as Promise Keepers have done, it is a shame they have been too timid to confront the issue of worldly amusements. This failure to shun evil amusements will eventually lead to much stumbling of men whose impure minds will find the promises of fidelity hard to keep. On the battlefield of moral purity, worldly amusements are a strong fortification of the enemy. The bodies of Christian brothers lie strewn about the field in front of the guns of Hollywood, their wives and children lying close behind!

Advice to Women

Sometimes when I speak to individuals or groups about the current entertainment situation, I like to ask the following question: "Can you think of one well-known movie actress today whose very name brings to mind purity, virtue, and the glory of feminine modesty? Just one?" There is usually a strange silence following this question. Of course, Old Hollywood had many such performers. A number of women developed their whole professional careers combining artistic excellence and moral virtue. A few examples would include Greer Garson, Loretta Young, June Allyson, Teresa Wright, and in a different sense, Katharine Hepburn. It is difficult even to mentally associate these women with shameful behavior on the screen. Yet, they had great presence, true talent, and were never dull. Old Hollywood certainly had its share of "bad girls" and vixens, but there were many actresses whose screen characters exuded virtue. What actress can make that claim today? And if none truly can, why are we idolizing these people? Why are we rushing to see them? Supporting them? Exposing our children to their shameful mouths and actions?

Traditionally, women have been the culture's guardians of virtue. Proper ladies were always modest. Bad language never came out of their mouths. Men might resort to vulgarity and impurity among themselves, but all of that changed in the presence of "the ladies." Men, in the company of women (what was called "mixed company") found themselves in an environment, a human context, in which they were mindful of moral constraints. Women represented morality, civilization, and self-control. Of course, this idea has died since women decided to join men in their coarseness and vulgarity. Many women who profess Christ in our day have not been able to find their way back to the role of custodian of virtue. The movies are part of this problem.

There are no cinematic role models for Christian women today. None. Yet, like Christian men, women patronize Hollywood's immoral displays as much as men. Many bring their men, and even their children, right into situations they should never be exposed to. It is women, along with teenagers, who made *Titanic* such a huge success. The reason for this may be that a woman's nature is more vulnerable to rank sentimentality. In such movies, tears rather than virtue define quality. Just as men compromise good morals for thrills, women compromise for sentiment. Hollywood consistently uses the manipulation of feelings to make immorality seem acceptable.

Women, return to virtue. When you slide into the muck with the rest of the culture, all is lost. When you cease to be offended or bothered by that which is impure and corrupt, there is little hope for your husbands and children.

Advice to Young People

I cannot offer advice to the teenager without offering an apology first. On behalf of my generation, I am deeply sorry you are growing up in a pornographic culture. I am grieved that you have no popular models of moral purity, no heroes who are virtuous and that you have never seen (beyond, perhaps, your own home) what it means to respect and honor women. If I could chop off an arm to change it, I would. But we are stuck with it. It is a burden you will have to bear. The mess we've made will probably never heal. Sometimes societies get so bad that God has to erase them. Yet, even in a world where the shameful is celebrated, there is still the cause of our Savior. Jesus Christ has us here on a mission. We are ambassadors. We represent His kingdom in our home, at our school, and in our community. We are, in His words, light in the darkness.

Back in the 1960s our society changed dramatically. Traditional morals founded on the Bible were overthrown for "drugs, sex, and rock-'n'-roll." It was a young-people's movement. They called the movement "counter-culture." It was directed against our civilization as it existed then. It's a different world now. Today, moral evil *is* the culture. Big businesses and artists devote their energies to evil. They mock the Bible and what it stands for. They seduce people with noise, thrills, and sex. They despise moral innocence. Good is laughed at, while evil is called good. It is a time of confusion and deep darkness.

The Christian teen of today has a duty to be "counter-culture." "You are the light of the world," Jesus said. You are the world's only hope. You must be a rebel for God.

Your heart, mind and soul must oppose the ways of the world. "Be as wise as serpents," the Lord said, "and innocent as doves." You cannot have one foot in God's kingdom and one foot in the world. The paths go off in different directions, and your legs are only so long. You must choose Christ, or you will lose the opportunity God has granted you to make a difference for Him.

The movies are aimed at you—the American teenager. People between the ages of twelve and twenty make up 16 percent of the population but 26 percent of moviegoers. This means that Hollywood tailors its films to appeal to you. Unfortunately, this means they not only appeal to your interests, but also to your weaknesses.

Hollywood wants to take advantage of your interest in the opposite sex; your desire to know "adult things"; your tricky, up-and-down emotions; your feelings of being held back by adult rules. Moviemakers could choose to help you through these times with some wisdom and understanding. Instead, they exploit your vulnerability in order to make a lot of money. They tease you, thrill you, and feed the lower part of your nature. They do this because it is good business. They care nothing for God. Nothing. You represent great, big dollar signs in Hollywood and nothing else. Corrupting people's morals has become profitable. Money rules.

If you have seen many modern films, you have seen and heard many things you should not have. You have been in bedrooms, the backseat of cars, bathrooms, and strip clubs. You have been given many peeps through the keyhole. You have been put in the position of a voyeur—a pervert who peeks through people's windows. The innocent, pure heart, which God treasures, has been corrupted. You must fight to get it back.

God is in the business of renewal. He cleanses and purifies, but we must be 100 percent for Him. Shun the impure and immodest. Turn it off. Keep away. Develop a taste for what is good. Love what God loves. Grieve over what grieves Him. That is the key to living the Christian life. Love Him more and you will love the impure less. Look about you. Do you see your friends struggling with purity and self-control? The battle is in the mind and heart. Victory or failure comes long before the test of actually being alone together with someone. Read the following scripture:

> Finally, brethren, whatever is true, whatever is honorable, whatever is right, whatever is pure, whatever is lovely, whatever is of good repute, if there is any excellence and if anything worthy of praise, let your mind dwell on these things. (Phil. 4:8)

Can you honestly say your entertainment choices are in line with this text? Where does your mind dwell?

Boys, you have no right to see women you are not married to undressed. God forbids that because he wants your heart to be devoted to one woman someday. He knows what such images do to your mind, your self-control. When you feed your mind on the flesh, you are charging your sexual batteries, which God designed for your marriage. It is foolish to feed your lusts. The Bible says you are treat "younger women as sisters, in all purity." I think the application to immodest entertainment is obvious. If you think something on the screen would be wrong for your sister to do, you should not be there watching yourself. Don't think, *I can handle it*. Better men than you have ruined their lives—and other's lives—by compromising what their eyes saw. Be honest with yourself. Find the courage to turn away from moral pollution.

Girls, the moviemakers know you want romance. Because they themselves delight in sin, they mix those longings with impurity. They want to make you comfortable with immodesty. They want you to laugh at perversion. They want to make you weep in sympathy for sin. Hollywood tells you over and over that good girls are not virgins. Love means sex. The Bible says such ideas are empty and deceitful. "Let no one deceive you with empty words," says the apostle, "for because of these things the wrath of God comes upon the sons of disobedience" (Eph. 5:8).

Hollywood creates ideal moments of perfect romantic sensuality on the screen, such as rarely exist in real life. They want to make you a woman of easy virtue, a loose woman. Look around you. How many girls do you know who are already giving in to sexual pressures? How many are already more devoted to romance than to God? Hollywood-style love is an idol and a cruel trap for those who worship before it. The truth is, Hollywood doesn't know what love is. The people who make the movies can rarely stay married for more than a few years themselves. Seek God's way, and don't fill your mind with evil. Also, girls, protect the boys. Don't let them see things they shouldn't. Be modest yourself, and let your entertainment choices be modest as well. You wouldn't give a young man you were interested in a subscription to *Playboy*, would you? Many films, even many PG and PG-13 films, have the same purpose and effect. A whole world out there needs your example of virtue.

Advice to Ministers

My brother pastors, it is time to shake off our lethargy and our own compromises. We must rouse ourselves to take on this issue of immoral entertainment. Our people are swimming in moral pollution, desperately in need of a word from God. Studies reveal that Christians watch the same movies and television shows as the general public, only they add religious films to their viewing patterns. Christians are just as much of the world as their pagan neighbors. This is a tragic state of affairs, and the responsibility for it is largely ours. Silent pulpits give free reign to sin. It's time to realize that speaking out against pornography is useless when PG, PG-13, and R-rated filth is far more common and, thus, more destructive. That is where your people get hooked. That is where their hearts are conformed to the world. The word *pornography* means "to write about or illustrate sexual licentiousness." That defines about 90 percent of Hollywood's product each year.

Amazingly, when I started warning people about the immorality of the movie *Titanic*, I was told by numerous people that some pastors in our area were actually encouraging their congregations to see it. Youth groups were going to see it on outings. One man in my church was told by a Christian friend that *Titanic* would change his life. Thankfully, he opted out of that change. This is how far the world has co-opted the church. We must pray for mercy. Then we must pray for boldness.

It is your duty, pastor, to be informed of the Bible's teaching on these matters. Wrestle with God's Word on this. Formulate a clear understanding of it. Then teach. You will offend some people, but you will give aid and deliverance to many others. Your people are longing for guidance. Don't preach platitudes and a vague morality. Your people can hear all of that and never apply it to their lives. Be specific. Let God break your heart over the sin of your people and the sin of our culture (see Dan. 9).

We are told by Christians who have Hollywood connections that we should be doing positive things to change Hollywood rather than spending our time and energy "Hollywood bashing." Frankly, Hollywood deserves bashing by anyone interested in righteousness. We are told by some brothers that our negative reactions to Hollywood's filth somehow diminishes our impact with the gospel in Hollywood. This is pure nonsense.

I'm actually a positive sort of guy, myself. No one rejoices more than I do when Hollywood comes out with something that is both wholesome and excellent. But that rejoicing is extremely rare. Outside of movies for very young children, Hollywood no longer makes more than one or two movies a year that merit Christian patronage. This track record does not deserve our praise. But when the rare good film comes out, made with a good message and wholesome methods, I tell my flock.

I believe in positive steps. I went to the local video store in town and offered to buy for the store video copies of movies I approve. My idea was to set up a Pastor's Corner where believers could rent wholesome films of quality. I had written reviews of the films from a Christian perspective, including questions for family discussion, which I would keep in supply. I offered to pay all the expenses and let the store keep all the revenues. Unfortunately, the store's owner turned me down, but I was happy to make the offer. It was a testimony to the store owner. It was a positive action.

But many voices in the evangelical community would tell me I am too negative. I don't trust those voices. When I am told to refrain from "bashing" the movie industry, I consider it a voice from the darkness. This all-pervasive source of sin and moral rot attacks the flock under my care. These media-loving Christians who want me to hold my tongue are not shepherds. We are shepherds, and it is our Master's flock. We cannot compromise.

The people in my town describe the residents of our community as a collection of firefighters, police officers, and Hollywood people. A few of the many movie people in our area attend our church. But I don't hide from these dear folks God's standard for the entertainment industry, anymore than I hide from our police officers God's standard for perfect integrity in law enforcement. I must proclaim the standard as God revealed it for every member of my flock. I don't despise people who work in Hollywood; indeed, I sympathize greatly with the hard choices which must be made every day by believers working in an industry devoted to sin. I've met producers and actors who have come to Christ. Truthfully, most of them end up doing something else. One former producer is now a chaplain in the air force. I admire his decision greatly. Can a Christian work in Hollywood? Yes, but at a sacrifice of either professional opportunities or his personal integrity. There is no middle ground.

The sad fact is that Christians in Hollywood have had about as much impact on the film industry as Lot had on Sodom. If anything, believers in Hollywood have profoundly lowered their standards in order to be accepted. Christian groups lavish praise on and even hand out awards to films that give any kind of approving nod to Christian beliefs, even if the film grossly violates any sense of decency in telling the story. That's how pitiful we have become. We are dogs begging crumbs of acceptance from the wrong table. I don't believe we need to be quite so desperate for the praise of the world that we forsake our Master's standards to side with those who exploit performers. Pastors, don't take your cues from those who have pitched their tents toward Sodom. Let the Bible be your unchanging standard.

Advice to Hollywood

I realize that these words will probably never be seen by anyone of importance in Hollywood, which is fine. But if I could communicate anything to those who run this industry, I would say two things. First, a spiritual point: eternity is a long time. You should read very carefully the words of Matthew 18:4–7. It is not a difficult passage to understand. It says that if you cause someone, especially a child or a weak soul, to lose his or her innocence—if you push that tender heart in the direction of sin—you will suffer sorrow such as you cannot comprehend in this world. Your only hope is repentance—turning from your grievous sins to the Savior whose laws you have mocked. That is the truth of it.

Second, a practical suggestion: Hollywood did just fine under the production code of 1934. But you have alienated many, many people from the movies. Each year, more and more people forsake the theater, and even television. Filth often is profitable, to be sure. You do succeed with trash. But why not broaden your appeal? Why not reinstate the production code for a certain percentage of your product? Every year you churn out dozens of movies that fail dismally; why not innovate? As an experiment that would likely generate for you lots of money, why not produce 5 to 10 percent of your movies under the old code? No, I don't mean movies for four year olds. I mean grown-up movies. You know, like those great movies of yesteryear that people still enjoy. Think Jimmy Stewart, and you'll start to have the idea. Offer filmmakers a production code option. No bad language, no sex talk, no naked bodies, no fornicating heroes—just great stories. I assure you there are hundreds of great stories out there. Many great adventures have never been told in the cinema. Wonderful books have never been tapped for their excellent stories. Talented writers are full of marvelous ideas. (Have you ever peeked into the great success of Focus on the Family's *Adventures in Odyssey*? There's a big market out there you are missing.) Find some clever marketing name for these "code" movies. You'll have to lure people who have forsaken the movies back in. It will take time, but why not bring back the code in a limited way as a test, for a limited period—say, five years. I think you would be surprised at the results.

Final Thoughts

For many Christians today, the movies exert something like the power of a vice. No matter how bad Hollywood's products get, many of us seem unable to give them up. As with all

vices, the cinema enthusiast convinces himself that the benefits, the pleasures, outweigh the dangers. The immediate gratification granted by cinematic thrills and weepy sentiment over-
whelm any serious moral consideration. We willingly accommodate ourselves to the world and its shamelessness.

I know that many cinema addicts will dismiss all that I
have labored to express in this book as just another attempt to
"curse the darkness" instead of offering light. If I am cursing
the darkness; it's about time. Every Christian book on the
movies I have seen in the last twenty years celebrates, at some
level, the darkness. We are told that because we may encounter faint sparks of light, we may enter the darkness at will. We
may partake of the world's offerings, especially if the world has
packaged its evil with great skill.

I have no interest in just cursing the darkness. My concern is dispelling the darkness. My current objective is even
more basic than that: simply calling the darkness what it is.
The problem today is fuzzy vision. We don't seem to know
where the darkness ends and the light begins. My mind harks
back to the ancient words of Isaiah: "If they do not speak
according to this word, it is because they have no dawn."
The Bible speaks, but do we hear it?

I know that in our day, the high-standards view of amusements I have described is a minority position. Tenaciously
and tenderly, Christian hearts cling to the twisted pleasures
of the movies. I understand it. I have felt the pull myself. I
love the cinema as a great art form. But for all its beauty and
power, I love God more. Compared to Him, the lure of Hollywood grows very dim. It is not a difficult choice: as far as

Hollywood rejects the Lord and the things He holds precious, I reject Hollywood.

We have let our King down. Commissioned as ambassadors of His Kingdom of light, we have grown fond of the darkness. In many ways, it seems too late for change. But although Hollywood's influence is uniquely pervasive, it is not more powerful than our Lord. I can say with hope that the world has been bad before, but the power that animated the church in other centuries is still available to us. The Holy Spirit lives. If we do not quench His power by continuing to honor and celebrate sin, we may yet rescue our culture. Certainly we will do better by our Lord, not to mention our children.

The Scripture describes the church as the bride of Christ. Our Lord died to make His bride pure. Paul said He

> gave Himself up for her; that He might sanctify her, having cleansed her by the washing of water with the word, that He might present to Himself the church in all her glory, having no spot or wrinkle or any such thing; but that she should be holy and blameless.

Any husband would desire not only physical purity, but just as much, and perhaps even more, mental purity—the complete devotion of mind and heart. With this in mind, patient reader, let me ask you to turn now from this book to a time of meditation and prayer regarding your entertainment choices.

Endnotes

CHAPTER ONE

1. Quoted by Francis A. Schaeffer, *The Great Evangelical Disaster* (Westchester, Ill: Crossway Books, 1984), pp. 50–51.

CHAPTER THREE

1. Philip Schaff, *History of the Christian Church* (1920 reprint, Grand Rapids: Wm. B. Eerdmans Publishing Company, 1980), II, p. 339.
2. Will Durant, *Caesar and Christ* (New York: Simon and Schuster, 1944), pp. 378–79.
3. Tertullian, *The Shows*, trans. by S. Thelwell, Ed. Alexander Roberts and James Donaldson, The Ante-Nicene Fathers (Grand Rapids: Wm. B. Eerdmans Publishing Company, 1986) III, p. 87
4. Menucius Felix, *The Octavius of Minucius Felix*, trans. By Ernest Wallis, Ed. Alexander Roberts and James Donaldson, The Ante-Nicene Fathers (Grand Rapids: Wm B. Eerdmans Publishing Company, 1986), IV, p. 196.

5. Cyprian, *On the Public Shows*, trans. by Ernest Wallis, Ed. Alexander Roberts and James Donaldson, The Ante-Nicene Fathers (Grand Rapids: Wm B. Eerdmans Publishing Company, 1986), V, p. 577.

6. Lactantius, *The Divine Institutes*, trans. by William Fletcher, Ed. Alexander Roberts and James Donaldson, The Ante-Nicene Fathers (Grand Rapids: Wm. B. Eerdmans Publishing Company, 1986), VII, p. 187.

7. John Chrysostom, *Homilies on Thessalonians*, trans. by John Broadus, Ed. Philip Schaff, The Nicene and Post-Nicene Fathers (Grand Rapids: Wm B. Eerdmans Publishing Company, 1983), XIII, p. 347.

8. Brian Edwards, *Shall We Dance? Dance and Drama in Worship* (Durham, England: Evangelical Press, 1991, rpt.), p. 37.

9. Bruce C. Daniels, *Puritans at Play: Leisure and Recreation in Colonial New England* (New York: St. Martin's Press, 1995), p. 68.

10. Richard Baxter, *A Christian Directory* (Morgan: Soli Deo Gloria Publications, 1996), p. 388.

11. Blaise Pascal, *Pascal's Pensees* (New York: E. P. Dutton and Company, Inc., 1958), p. 5.

12. William Wilberforce, *A Practical View of the Prevailing Religious System of Professed Christians, in the Higher and Middle Classes in this Country, Contrasted with Real Christianity* (Philadelphia: Key and Biddle, 1835), pp. 226–27.

13. John Wesley, *The Message of the Wesleys*, Compiled by Philip S. Watson (New York: The MacMillan Company, 1964), p. 189.

14. G. William Jones, *Sunday Night at the Movies* (Richmond: John Knox Press, 1967), p. 27.

15. Arthur Knight, *The Liveliest Art* (New York: The MacMillan Company, 1957), p. 111.

16. Greer Garson, quoted in *Newsweek*, 15 April, 1996, p. 64.

17. Lawrence Murray, *The Celluloid Persuasion* (Grand Rapids: William B. Eerdmans Publishing Company, 1979), p. 39.

18. John R. Rice, *What is Wrong with the Movies?* (Grand Rapids: Zondervan Publishing House, 1938), p. 13.

19. Ibid., pp. 96–97

20. Herbert J. Miles, *Movies and Morals* (Grand Rapids: Zondervan Publishing House, 1947).

21. Harry J. Jaeger, *What About the Movies?* Religious Tract reprinted from "The Sunday School Times", circa 1943.
22. Josh McDowell and Bob Hostetler, *Right From Wrong* (Dallas: Word Publishing, 1994), pp. 93–94.
23. Mike Yorkey, "Christian Film Critics Urge Moviegoers to Seek Guidance," *Citizen*, January 1989, p. 7.

CHAPTER FIVE

1. Dorothy Sayers, *The Whimsical Christian* (New York: Collier Books, 1987), p. 114.
2. Frank Getlein and Harold Gardiner, *Movies, Morals, and Art* (New York: Sheed and Ward, 1961), p. 105.
3. Frank E. Gaebelein, *The Christian, The Arts, and Truth*, ed. D. Bruce Lockerbie (Portland: Multnomah, 1985), p. 52.
4. Harold Gardiner, *Movies, Morals, and Art*, p. 114.
5. Newsweek, December 15, 1997.
6. Blaise Pascal, *Pascal's Pensees*, Trans. by T. S. Eliot (New York: E. P. Dutton,1953), pp. 114–15.
7. Romans 1:18.
8. Neil P. Hurley, *Toward a Film Humanism* (New York: Dell Publishing Co., 1975, rpt) pp. 66–67.
9. Harold Gardiner, *Movies, Morals, and Art*, p. 106.
10. Ibid., pp. 106–107.
11. 1 Thessalonians 5:2.

CHAPTER SEVEN

1. Frank Getlein and Harold Gardiner, *Movies, Morals, and Art* (New York: Sheed and Ward, 1961), p. 153.
2. William Wilberforce, *A Practical View of the Prevailing Religious System of Professed Christians, in the Higher and Middle Classes in this Country, Contrasted with Real Christianity* (Philadelphia: Key and Biddle, 1835), pp. 231–232.
3. Franky Schaeffer, *Sham Pearls for Real Swine* (Brentwood, TN: Wolgemuth and Hyatt Publishers, Inc., 1990) pp. 56–57.

4. Marilyn Beck, "Madsen Just Says No to a TV Nude Scene," Column, *The Daily News*, 28 Feb., 1991.
5. Basset quoted in *Satellite Orbit*, September 1998, p. 332.
6. O'Grady quoted by Eirek Knutzen, "Nomination Gives O'Grady Bigger Roles," *Antelope Valley Press*, 20 July, 1995, Section B, p. 4.
7. Melanie McLean Michel, "My Mother's Best Advice," USA Weekend, 12-12 May, 1995, p. 8.
8. Susan Brill, "Actors Who Just Say No," *Christianity Today*, July 15, 1996, p. 53.

Chapter Eight

1. Augustine Confessions, Book VI, Chapter eight.
2. Laurent Bouzereau, *Ultra Violent Movies*, (New York: Citadel Press, 1996).
3. Laurent Bouzereau, p. 44.
4. Ibid. p. 67.
5. Ibid. p. 35.
6. Ibid. p. 69.
7. Ibid. p. 130.
8. Basset quoted in *Satellite Orbit*, September 1998, p. 332.

Chapter Ten

1. Neil Postman, *The Disappearance of Childhood* (New York: Vintage Books, 1994), p. 44.
2. Eric Schlosser, "The Business of Pornography," U.S. News and World Report, 10 Feb. 1997, pp. 43–49.
3. Bill McCartney, "Legacy of Purity," *The Promise Keeper*, July/August 1998, p. 2.

Chapter Twelve

1. America Online's *Kids in Mind*, Critics, Inc., 1998.
2. Amy Wallace, "The Coming PG-13 Juggernaut," *Los Angeles Times*, 7 October 1997, sec. F.

3. Ibid.
4. Ibid.

CHAPTER THIRTEEN

1. K. L. Billingsley, *The Seductive Image* (Westchester, Ill :Crossway Books, 1989), p. 23.
2. Ibid., pp. 21–22.
3. Ibid., p. 21.
4. Ibid., p. xi.
5. Lael F. Arrington, *World Proofing Your Kids* (Wheaton: Crossway Books, 1997), p. 260.
6. Joel Belz, "Why Do We Tolerate Simulation When the Real Thing's Not Allowed?" *AFA Journal*, Nov/Dec, 1997, p. 19

CHAPTER FOURTEEN

1. Franky Schaeffer, *Sham Pearls for Real Swine* (Brentwood, Tennesee: Wolgemuth and Hyatt, Publishers, Inc.,1990), p.245.
2. Ibid., p.22.
3. Ibid., p.135.
4. Ibid., pp. 50, 82, 130.
5. Ibid., pp. 38, 111.
6. Ibid., p.131
7. Bruce C. Daniels, *Puritans at Play: Leisure and Recreation in Colonial New England* (New York: St. Martin's Press, 1995), p. 66.
8. Schaeffer, *Sham Pearls for Real Swine*, p.16.
9. Ibid., p. 174.
10. Ibid., p.121.
11. C. H. Spurgeon, *The Soul Winner* (Springdale, PA: Whitaker House, 1995), pp. 261–262.
12. Francis A. Schaeffer, *How Should We Then Live?* (Old Tappan, NJ: Fleming H. Revell Company, 1976), p. 71.
13. Frank Getlein and Harold Gardiner, *Movies, Morals, and Art* (New York: Sheed and Ward, 1961), p. 96.

CHAPTER FIFTEEN

1. Franky Schaeffer, *Sham Pearls for Real Swine* (Brentwood, Tennesee: Wolgemuth and Hyatt, Publishers, Inc.,1990), p. 9.
2. Ibid., p. 9.
3. Frank E. Gaebelein, *The Christian, The Arts, and Truth*, ed. D. Bruce Lockerbie (Portland: Multnomah, 1985), p. 113.
4. Neil Postman, *The Disappearance of Childhood* (New York: Vintage Books, 1994), pp. 83–84.
5. Schaeffer, *Sham Pearls for Real Swine*, p. 111.
6. Joseph Sobran, "The Bare, and Real, Facts about Nudity in Films," Editorial, The Daily News, February 6, 1986.
7. Schaeffer, *Sham Pearls for Real Swine*, p. 59.
8. Amos Vogel, *Film as a Subversive Art* (New York: Random House, 1974), p. 201.

Movie Index

Scripture Index

The author of *Worldly Amusements* welcomes reader comments and criticism. He can be reached at:

c/o Acton Faith Bible Church
P. O. Box 398
Acton, CA 93510